Better Vacations

for Your Money

BETTER
VACATIONS
FOR YOUR MONEY

By MICHAEL FROME

With a Foreword by CONRAD WIRTH
Director National Park Service

DOUBLEDAY & COMPANY, INC.
Garden City, New York

Contents

Foreword

Leisure-time travel in recent years has become a major factor in the American way of life. Never before in our history have so many Americans had the opportunity, and the means, to move so far afield and enjoy the scenic beauty, the historic resources, and the rewarding recreational delights of our nation.

As travel becomes more convenient, however, it also becomes more complex. Helpful advice at the start of a trip can mean the difference between a journey of frustrating disappointments and one of sheer delight.

Michael Frome, from his long experience in the field of travel, is eminently qualified to advise and suggest to the inexperienced as well as the experienced traveler the ways and means of getting the most out of every journey.

To the National Park Service, Michael Frome is more than a travel expert—he is a good friend. In Washington he has given us valued counsel and assistance. In many field areas, park personnel from superintendents to seasonal rangers know and respect him.

The national parks have felt the effect of the rising tide in recreational travel, with an astounding increase in visitors, now totaling almost 60 million a year. We are presently in the midst of a 10-year program, Mission 66, designed to provide improved services and facilities which the park visitor has the right to expect, while assuring the lasting preservation and protection of our national treasures. Our completion target is 1966, the fiftieth anniversary of the establishment of the National Park Service.

Many other areas, under federal, state, and local administration, as well as private ownership, form the fabric of America's vacationland. One of the many useful features of this book is the presentation of the broad range of places to go and activities to enjoy. There is no limit to the possibilities in America.

I join the author in wishing you interesting reading through this guide, and happy journeys to follow.

Conrad L. Wirth, Director
National Park Service

**Better Vacations
for Your Money**

Mobility, a modern freedom, enables everyone to explore America. The magnificent vista of Oregon's Pacific Coast, seen here south of Cannon Beach, is now within reach of any starting point during the course of a planned vacation.

1

Luxury at Low Cost—
the Modern Vacation Formula

Yesterday's concept of going places in America is about as outmoded as yesterday's concept of almost any phase of the American scene.

Excitement, change, freshness—a newness comparable to the pioneer opening of the West—are abroad in the land. Travel in one direction and you see new cities changing the landscape. In another direction old cities are being reshaped and practically born anew. You find dams and mammoth recreational lakes where none existed the last time you went by. And roads penetrate once inaccessible forestland to open the rich natural resources of mountains, streams, valleys and canyons.

Now you can recast your thinking of what vacation travel means to you and your family. Prepare for new ideas, new places to visit, greater distances within your reach, more rewarding experiences. Plus a taste of genuine luxury at low cost.

This book is designed to help you chart your course, although I hope you will not find it a "how-to" guide in the usual sense. Practical pointers are important and many are included. But please do not accept them simply to save money. They are all calculated to add to the fun of going places.

If saving were the only consideration, the best solution would be to stay home, which, incidentally, costs money, too. We Americans, however, are not built that way. Not with a big beautiful country like ours asking to be seen, appreciated, and enjoyed. Nor with the mobility afforded by our motor cars and modern highway system.

It is simply too late in history to counsel against vacation travel—or to insist that one wait until he is old or wealthy enough to afford it. Travel is a characteristic of our time and of our standard of living. Somewhere lies the route to a thoroughly delightful trip for every family (and the unattached), the rich, poor, and middling. The objective in the following pages is to help you find yours.

Getting away from our own narrow corners is a good thing to do for our state of mind and health, individually and collectively. As most doctors advise, the proper combination of change of scenery and climate will ease the pressures on body and mind, even add years to your life. No, it won't do to spend the time at home; you must reflect new pictures in the mirror of your mind. Weekend trips and long holidays are fine, but try to plan one vacation a year of at least two weeks so you feel you're really getting away from it all. The net result of such a trip will be renewed vigor and renewed appreciation of the world, its natural ways, and the people with whom you share it. The odds are that any man who enjoys a vacation with his wife will rediscover her glamour—and she probably needs the respite from routine much more than he does. Even if you can farm out the children, my counsel is that you take them along so they can discover that parents are down-right human and fun to be with.

Does this have anything to do with the amount of money you spend? Well, yes. And then again, perhaps not as much as you think.

The value—or purchasing power—of a dollar is immensely relative, isn't it? If you are traveling on an expense account, it is negligible. The same if you are a businessman who can charge the trip to your business. But if you are spending your own hard-earned cash, the money becomes measurably more significant. With a dollar at some restaurants you can scarcely buy more than a roll, a pat of butter, and a cup of coffee, yet elsewhere a dollar feeds a family of three or four.

The magic vacation formula is in the combination of frugality and luxury. Frugality because for most of us it is necessary these days and waste, under any circumstances, is foolish. Luxury because you deserve and need it on a vacation. Happily, we have been endowed with and own so much of the finest that all we need do is open our eyes to see and experience luxury. Independence of judgment is also important, which means that if you think camping is for the birds and the bears you ought to leave it strictly to them and plan your vacation otherwise.

Remember that big money does not guarantee a happy vacation, just as it does not guarantee happiness in life. Some people stay at the finest hotels and dine at the most expensive restaurants, not because they really want to, but out of compulsion. They never deviate from the standard course if they can help it, and usually do very little they couldn't have done equally as well at home. They discover little that is new or different, or even restful, because they are eternally pressed by the need for ostentation and the collection of conversation pieces.

The wise traveler will shed artificiality and search for more genuine things. Inexpensive vacationing can be a much deeper, richer, and finer experience. There is a world of difference between a low-cost trip and a cheap trip. The real values depend far less on budget than on

The Natchez Trace Parkway, Mississippi, is the type of road designed for the sport of touring.

your outlook. Start with the concept of travel as an adventure so individualized that only you and your family can plot your course. Your trip should be an expression of contemporary freedom and your refined taste.

The motor car is part of the pattern. You are the skipper. The *Queen Mary* may be larger, but its captain has no more authority over his vessel than you have over yours. He cannot stop between one shore and the other, but you can put into port and set sail wherever and whenever you choose. Nor does your car have to be the largest, latest model—consider it first-class transportation regardless of size or vintage. For your children the family car represents a classroom on wheels, enabling them to touch geography and history, giving these studies a living meaning far beyond the textbook scope. For us all, motoring opens the heart of America to our sight and perception.

Sure, you are going to spend money on your trip, though in this book you should find many ways to get more value for your dollars. I will show you, for example, how to select the type of accommodations best suited to your family, at the lowest possible cost . . . how to get the most out of a camping trip, whether you have ever tried it before or not . . . the full range in public recreation areas, with maps to spot many of their locations . . . the open door to a host of free travel services and low-cost touring attractions . . . how to make motoring a pleasure, rather than a pain . . . how to budget for your vacation . . . the way to buy quality souvenirs for less money. You will also find a series of itineraries covering money-saving vacation areas from the restful wilderness to the zestful city.

All of this represents the distillation of ideas and counsel furnished by friends and collaborators—federal officials, national forest supervisors and national park superintendents, travel editors, state travel directors, automobile club managers, oil companies, industries large and small. Credit them if you save money. And you should save at least ten times the cost of the book for each week of your vacation.

But don't weigh money values alone. I have deliberately coupled the element of appreciation with economy. Follow this course and expect your preception of travel sights to deepen from eye level to mind level.

Above all, start with the happy conviction that you are planning a quality vacation. As for the money you spend, set forth with the feeling that this is scarcely the time to be niggardly, but do not hesitate to temper generosity with discrimination and judgment. This combination will take you farther and bring you home with more lasting satisfaction.

Where is Vacationland? Americans find it at rocky, surf-splashed Great Head, Maine, along Ocean Drive.

South of Nags Head, North Carolina, is sandy Coquina Beach, on the new road to Cape Hatteras.

In Mammoth Cave, Kentucky, crossing Echo River, 350 feet below the surface . . .

High above Cascade Canyon—and still looking upward!—to Grand Teton, Wyoming, 13,700 feet.

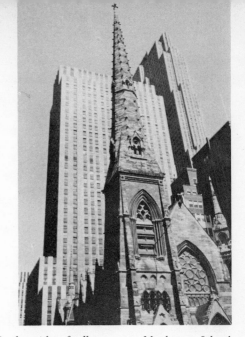

In the midst of tall towers on Manhattan Island.

Among the quiet giants of the California redwood forest.

You meet new friends on vacation, like the white-tailed deer fawn in Lolo National Forest, Idaho.

And the venerable Smoky Mountaineer, of Cades Cove, Tennessee, showing how he keeps swarms of bees in hollowed gum trees, called "bee gums."

2

Plan Now,
Play Later

Planning is an essential element of a successful vacation. The more time and effort you invest in planning, the greater your dividends will be. To determine where you are going, how you will get there, and where you will stay once you arrive are the first steps to travel enjoyment and economy.

It sounds simple and elementary, doesn't it? Yet millions of good people set out unknowing and unplanned, like chronic gypsies. Their haphazard mobility proves unrewarding, costly, and often frustrating. Follow such a course and you are apt to run into circumstances like these:

· You drive a hundred miles more than you expected before finding a night's lodging. Result, children unhappy, wife unhappy, next day (at least) shot.

· You arrive in a crowded resort area, where all accommodations are filled, end up paying twice as much as necessary.

· Your money runs out before you reach home.

· You drive past, or near, points of interest you learn about later and wish you had seen.

· You book reservations and when you arrive find the place is nothing like what you had in mind. The question then becomes, "How soon can we leave and where do we go from here?"

Forethought, intelligent planning, elimination of guesswork and question marks are easily managed. It doesn't matter whether you are embarking on a month-long trip or only a weekend away; think through your destination, route, cost. The secret in travel saving is in the care you take early, as opposed to spur-of-the-moment decisions. As a general rule, if you are going to be away from home one night plot out your trip one week in advance; if you are going to be away two nights, plan two weeks in advance. If you are going on a two-week trip, plan it six months in advance, and for a month-long trip start the wheels in motion one year early.

Time involved in planning a trip to Colonial Williamsburg deepens enjoyment of the visit. This exhibit, at the Information Center, depicts life in eighteenth-century Virginia.

As you begin your preliminary planning, be sure you follow these four steps:

1. *Assemble travel aids.* (See "Friends Who Help You Save.") "During my years in the Tourist Bureau," recalls Joseph A. Bursey, the former promotion director of New Mexico, "we had a great many letters from people who received our literature after they had visited our state. Invariably, they expressed regret that they hadn't received this material before their trips. Many people think of New Mexico as a desert, or as a place which is snowbound in winter. They don't realize that most of our points of interest are off the beaten path and that they must take side trips to see them. This is where proper preparation could be of tremendous help."

2. *Chart your itinerary.* A good set of maps is of paramount importance to every motorist, no matter how well he thinks he knows the roads. With the multibillion-dollar national highway program well

Forethought and preparation, not high spending, enable this family—even with a tiny infant—to have a happy vacation at Sequoia National Park, California.

underway, new roads—and detours—are popping up everywhere. Without an accurate map, preferably one marked by an expert, you are likely to encounter unexpected delays or bypasses, or to follow an old route when you might just as well use a new one. Spend a little time absorbing the meaning of map symbols, that is, the differences between expressways, state highways and other types of roads. Often, a straight line is not the shortest distance in travel time between two points. If you give a good map a chance, it will tell you the location of parks, forests, points of interest and campgrounds.

3. *Learn about the range in accommodations early.* (See "Give Mother a Break?") If you are going to a popular, crowded area, don't wait too long before placing your reservation. Writing at the strategic time helps, too. In Tennessee, where state park reservations are parceled out first come, first served, starting January 1, some early birds walk from their New Year's Eve parties to the post office.

4. *Study the area you intend to visit.* You can prepare for your trip

with background reading matter, either at your bookstore or local library. Try such books as River of Grass by Marjorie Stoneman Douglas, if you're going to the Everglades in Florida; the Great Smokies and Blue Ridge, edited by Roderick Peattie, for the Southern Appalachians; Bonanza Trail, by Muriel S. Wolle, the "bible" on present condition of ghost towns and mining camps of the West.

Don't confine your reading to guidebooks, but reach for a broader base. If you are motoring West, learn something about the history of western expansion from such books as Irving Stone's *Men to Match My Mountains,* one of the Mainstream of America Series. It will enliven your trip as you travel the route of the early explorers and covered wagon trains.

Carry along useful books to help you identify and understand wildlife, trees, minerals, geologic formations. Among those worth having are Roger Torrey Peterson's *Field Guides to Birds of Eastern United States and Western United States;* Doubleday's Pocket Nature Guides which include the *Audubon Land Bird Guide* by Richard H. Pough and the *Wild Flower Guide* by Edgar T. Wherry; the *Golden Nature Guides on Seashore, Trees, Flowers, Mammals, and the Southwest; Meet the Natives,* by M. Walter Pesman, a guide to trees, wildflowers and shrubs of the Rocky Mountains.

Children are the principal beneficiaries of pre-trip reading. Publications like the Garden City nature series which includes *THE STORY OF ROCKS* by Dorothy Shuttlesworth, *PLANTS OF WOODLAND AND WAYSIDE* by Su Zan Swain, and *THE WEB OF NATURE* by Ted Pettit and Don Ray; the Landmark series, Golden Nature Books and Audubon Junior News prepare them for the places they are to visit; remember, the more absorbed a youngster becomes in his trip the less of a problem he is to his parents.

Knowing whom to write and what literature to ask for are important. For publications on the federal areas, order from the Superintendent of Documents, Government Printing Office, Washington 25, D.C. (See "Everyman's Playground, the Public Lands.") These are the principal items of travel literature:

"Areas Administered by the National Park Service," 52 pages, thumbnail description of 180 areas, including outstanding characteristics and pertinent data. Price, 20¢.

"National Parks, Historic Sites, National Monuments," a catalog of government folders, booklets, and books from 5¢ to $2.25. The catalog is free.

Travelers who learn about Quebec in advance know they can stretch shopping dollars for duty-free woolens and chinaware imported from Britain.

The motorist who charts his itinerary finds time to scan the Virginia landscape from Shenandoah National Park, Virginia, instead of suffering endless hours behind the wheel.

For literature or information on a specific park area, write the Government Printing Office; the individual park leaflets cost 5–10¢. Then, if you need further information, write the superintendent of the park at his address.

"Camping Facilities in the National Park System," 24 pages, an alphabetical listing showing name and address of the area, name of the campground, number of camp sites; information on tables, benches, toilets, cooking facilities, drinking water, laundry facilities. Price, 15¢.

"National Park System, Eastern United States," "National Park System, Western United States." Large, useful planning maps, spotting all the park areas. Reverse side includes information on principal facilities and activities at each area. Price, 15¢ each.

"National Forest Vacations," an excellent 66-page introduction to the national forests, outlining them individually, their special features, recreation resources and attractions. Price, 30¢.

For a specific area, write the Forest Supervisor; for example, Forest Supervisor, Ocala National Forest, Florida. All addresses are listed in the booklet "National Forest Vacations." Folders are available (free) on the individual forests.

"Reclamation's Recreational Opportunities," a directory of 140 areas on reclamation projects and their facilities for water sports, camping, lodging, and hunting. Price, 15¢.

"Visiting National Wildlife Refuges," eight pages, outlining refuge functions, recreation possibilities, and overnight accommodations, where available. Price, 10¢. Leaflets on individual refuges are available free.

"Recreation on TVA Lakes," an excellent folder with map and directory of facilities in seven states. Write Tennessee Valley Authority, Knoxville, Tennessee.

For state parks, and state camping directories, write the State Parks Department at the capital of the state you plan to visit.

For general literature on attractions, highways and lodgings, write to State Tourist Promotion Bureau at the state capital. This is not always the precise name of the agency, but will suffice to reach it.

Oil companies and chambers of commerce (see "Friends Who Help You Save").

3

Tenting on the New Campground

If you haven't joined in the current camping boom, then you are missing the most mobile, least expensive means of vacationing in the American outdoors.

Women, though they don't expect to like it, take to camping with ease and prove better campers than men. Youngsters—especially those bred in cities and suburbs—become so absorbed with nature they are easy to handle and actually prove helpful.

Camping is the simplest kind of outdoor vacationing but by no means the only one. If you insist on sleeping in a bed in a room with a roof, that is precisely what you should do. Don't try camping only because it is inexpensive, but because you want to try camping. There are other moneysaving ways to take advantage of the outdoors, if only to pack a lunch to eat at a roadside park along the way.

But you need not be afraid to give camping a whirl. It is much easier than you think. In the past decade this great American pastime has skyrocketed in popularity, with more than 22 million tent-pitching campers last year. Throngs of city-bred novices have joined the ranks,

Camping, a national pastime. A state-operated camp site near Haines Falls in the Catskills, New York. Family expenses while tenting are often less than while living at home.

as enthusiastic and adept as the long-experienced countryman. Just start easily with a night out in your own back yard or close to home. Don't plan an extensive trip at the outset or purchase expensive equipment until you are sure that camping is to your liking. And do not look for savings immediately; considering your initial investment for equipment, you won't feel the real economy for two or three years.

Camping is considerably different from what it used to be. Twenty or thirty years ago it was close to being a frontier-type experience. Campers would travel along until they found a green valley alongside a river, pitch a tent and proceed to rough it. Camping today is easier and more pleasant. Instead of fighting with an old-fashioned fireplace, you can cook with a handy two-burner stove. Sleeping bags and bedrolls have been simplified and lightened so that even children can handle them. Clothing is lighter, too, and easier to wash. Tents have been refined with aluminized weatherproofing fabric and rodentproof flaps (see, Mother, no field mice tonight). Instead of sleeping on the

At the shore of Roosevelt Lake, Washington. Campers swim when they like, then dry their suits on convenient clotheslines. Of all vacationers, campers have the widest selection of places to visit.

ground, you make life pleasant with cots and light, compact air mattresses, and, rather than fight to set up tent poles and pegs, you open the latest model almost as simply as your umbrella. You can buy a tent to fit your car top or car back, ranging in color to flamboyant pink and even two tones. Food? Carry an insulated ice refrigerator with fresh butter, milk, and leafy vegetables, along with the light new packaged and powdered foods.

In the old days eating outdoors beneath a shade tree or beside a stream always involved a few thousand uninvited and unwelcome bugs. Now you use sprays or "bombs." Repellents to cope with mosquitoes have come a long way from citronella. There is such a thing as camping in style, and when you do, you're really traveling first class!

Campgrounds are much improved, with better fireplaces, comfort stations, showers. The newer campgrounds are less crowded and give more space to the individual units; the latest are also equipped with laundromats and bathhouses.

Who goes in for camping? Well, it is largely a family pursuit. Surveys show the average camping parties are composed of four persons —parents and two children. Campers are close to the average national family income of $5520. This means there are some richer than others (23 per cent earning above $7000) and some poorer (14 per cent earning under $3000). They are all pretty solid democratic-type Americans around a campground. And if it were not for camping some families could not vacation at all. For instance, one county high school principal, his wife, and four children spent the summer touring the western national parks. "Happily," he said, "we all love camping. If we didn't, we would have had to spend the summer at home."

A survey in Washington State showed that 60 per cent of campers in state parks were Washington residents, while the remainder came from 45 states, Canada, and other foreign nations. Washingtonians averaged 822 miles round trip; those from other states, 3200 miles, and from Canada, 1722 miles. The campers stayed 2.3 days in one park, 5.1 days in other parks. Many used other lodgings as well—35 per cent motel accommodations and 30 per cent staying with friends and relatives en route.

These figures are interesting for a first-time camper, since they indicate what to expect. The average spending in Washington was $7.43 per person per day and the trip total $150.61, ranging from $81.80 for Washington residents to $290.93 for those from other states. Most of all, they enjoyed the opportunity to be outdoors (72 per cent); second, the clean overnight accommodations (68 per cent); third, economy (58 per cent); and fourth, friendliness of park personnel (47 per cent). This shows the kind of people campers are: given a patch of sky and ground, they pitch their tent, step up to the ranger, and say, "Thank you." And he is just the kind of fellow who says, "Thank *you*" right back.

One third were on their first camping trip, so you can count on plenty of company. Most people intended not just to visit one park but to travel around Washington and the Northwest. And there, in flexibility, is camping's real advantage. You can select areas that offer fishing, hiking, riding, mountain climbing; you can visit the seashore or the woodlands, the cool mountains, the lake shores, be within walking distance of luxury resorts or in sheer isolation. And whereas the guest at Yosemite's Ahwahnee or the Lodge at Jackson Lake merely admires the scenery, you are living in it. As you grow more expert you will be able to go anywhere, from Florida to the Canadian Rockies and Alaska.

Just try camping once or twice, and you will probably be won over.

Fortunately, campgrounds are being expanded to handle the rising volume of business. The National Park Service is adding 20,000 more camp sites; the U. S. Forest Service and the states are adding thousands more (California alone has a program to double its 2700 camp sites). However, they are still not spaced evenly across the country— another important reason to plan your trip carefully.

As you get into camping you will gradually start looking for areas that are more isolated and more primitive. In touring, you don't have to camp out every night, but you can alternate with hotel and motel stops; the touch of added comfort will prove a welcome change.

What equipment do you need for camping and how much will it cost? The total will range anywhere from about $150 to $500 for a family of three or four. A large investment, but the materials are good for years. First of all, think of how you are going to sleep. Your biggest expense will be the tent. You are probably wiser to get something with head room, an attached canvas floor, a window opposite the door for ventilation, and a canopy front. The old reliable is the compact 8 by 8 tepee, or range tent, set up with two poles and pegs. The umbrella type is convenient and popular. You might look into the new pop tent (preferably the larger size) manufactured by the Pop Tent Corporation, Ann Arbor, Michigan. Held together with six fibre glass rods, it can be set up within two or three minutes. It has bug-proof zipper netting as well as a rear window. Whatever you get, try it in your yard several times before you start rolling.

Two very important items are your sleeping bag and air mattress. Do not try to purchase the cheapest, but those that will be light and compact, yet give you a comfortable night's rest.

Down is the warmest and lightest sleeping bag material, but if you have a feather allergy or sinus trouble it could prove all wrong for you. Kapok is less allergenic, dacron non-allergenic, but not as warm. Shop for what is called a "double bag" (that is, with an inside liner), equipped with a hood that can be used as a tent cover for your head —the night may come when you decide to sleep out, come stars or rain.

In buying a sleeping bag, remember that nylon is lighter than rubber. Choose a ribbed bag in which the air will be divided evenly, and try to get one that doesn't take much blowing effort, unless an air pump is part of your equipment. If you're inflating it by mouth, a mattress with plugs will probably be better than one with valves. Whatever you get, be careful not to overinflate; carry a supply of patches (DAB) so you are prepared for leaks. Another important item is a tarpaulin or polyethylene ground cover to place under your mattress; an army surplus poncho will serve this purpose, too. Cots are handy but not nearly as light as air mattresses.

BASIC CAMPING EXPENSES FOR A FAMILY OF FOUR

1 Tent, umbrella type with screen and ground cloth	$100
1 Car-top luggage rack (or one-wheel trailer $75)	15
4 Air mattresses	60
4 Sleeping bags	120
1 Propane or gasoline lantern (or kerosene lantern, $2)	10
1 Canvas sheet, 10' x 15', to shelter picnic table or outdoor camp in rain	15
1 Cook stove	15
Cooking kit	10
1 Set of eating utensils	5
1 Ax	5
2 Flashlights	3
4 Insect bombs	3.50
	$361.50

Take it easy when you shop. Talk to your friends, shop around, and learn while you do. Try the army surplus stores. Use things from your home to the maximum. Avoid expensive camp gadgets. Take along what you need to be comfortable, dry, and well fed. Some of the old-time campers prefer the fireplace to cook stove; the food tastes better, they say, and their load is lighter.

When you do start out camping, try to arrive early in the day if you're headed for a popular area so you can pick your spot before the crowds arrive. It will also take you a little longer to break camp and get rolling in the morning than if you were staying at a motel.

Trailer camping? It is booming along with tent camping, especially in the Western States. Manufacturers are now producing models ten feet wide (called tenwides) with enough space for two bedrooms, living room and kitchen seating four people. A number of states are relaxing their eight-foot restrictions and permitting the tenwides.

Trailer travel—particularly rental—has advantages of economy and comfort. If you were planning a Western vacation, for example, you could drive to Salt Lake City, rent a trailer and tour northward through the Wyoming, Idaho and Montana forests and parks. The cost of trailer rental ranges from $25 to $55 a week, depending on the model.

You will do best to select a short trailer, rather than one of the jumbos. Any car can pull a trailer up to 30 feet long, but a medium-to-heavy car is needed for anything longer. Write the Mobile Home Manufacturers Association, 20 North Wacker Drive, Chicago 6, Illinois, for the Travel and Vacation Trailer Park Guide (price 50¢). It lists rental dealers, commercial trailer parks, location of trailer campsites in public parks and forests.

Trailer vacationing is reaching such proportions that in some national forests fifty percent of available camping space is being developed for trailers, with the latest improvements in electric, sewer and water connections.

A health note: bring along a liberal supply of "Off" or "6-12," insect and mosquito repellants, in their various forms—bomb, stick, liquid—and use freely. Protect children from poison ivy by identifying the leaf for them so they can steer clear of it. Calamine lotion relieves itching but consult a doctor if it spreads.

Besides camping, there are other worth-while outdoor pursuits. Try walking. Some people do, despite a widespread attitude once enunciated by Fred Allen when he quipped: "I like long walks, especially when they are taken by people who annoy me." Walking is not only good fun, but a tonic for the mind and body; it stimulates the intake of fresh air and the flow of blood throughout the body.

You need not work at it as did Thoreau, who was proud to report he frequently "tramped eight or ten miles through the deepest snow to keep an appointment with a beech tree, or a yellow birch, or an old acquaintance among the pines." But walking is important as a means of enjoying vacation travel to the fullest. After all, you simply cannot see everything from the window of a car, even if it is rolled down. You may be able to say you have been to a place, but unless you apply some leg work along with tire consumption, you can't really say you have experienced it.

"We encourage visitors to get out of their cars and walk," John Doerr, chief naturalist of the National Park Service, points out. "Walking provides the opportunity for intimacy with things to be seen and heard; it makes possible a real understanding of plant life, animals, geology, and other distinct features found in the national parks. Even for the casual visitor, walking is encouraged at the lookouts and turnoffs along the roads in the parks. The best view is not always the one from the car, but walking a short distance often will bring it to the eye."

That is why the Park Service conducts some 20,000 walking trips a year, which anyone can join. These adventures range from an hour to an entire day and are conducted by expert, friendly naturalists. A number of unique walking trips can be made in the parks. In such places as Mammoth Cave, Wind Cave, and Carlsbad Caverns the visitor walks deep below the earth's surface. In Yosemite, the High Sierra trip takes a full week of walking through the mountain wilder

Walking: time well spent following the guided nature trail in Great Smoky Mountains National Park, Tennessee-North Carolina.

The long walk: a stop for the night at Hawksbill Shelter, Virginia, on the Appalachian Trail. The Trail extends 2000 miles from Mount Katahdin, Maine, to Mount Oglethorpe, Georgia.

ness at the rate of 12 to 18 miles a day with overnight stops at remote camps. The ultimate in thrills: guided mountain climbing in the Rocky Mountains, Mount Rainier, and the Grand Tetons. For experts, yes, but not exclusively; if you're in good health and can climb a flight of stairs, the guide can teach you to scale these towering American peaks. And you can rent the climbing equipment in the parks.

John Doerr, who has trod in many corners, was asked to name his most unusual experience afoot. "Hawaii," he replied. "The world's weirdest walk, they call it. You cover three miles down the wall of Kilauea crater, across the crater floor, beyond fantastic lava formations, to the fire pit. It is called Halemaumau, the "house of everlasting fire," and when it boils with molten lava it looks it. You don't walk then!"

It isn't necessary to visit Hawaii, or even the national parks and forests, to find worth-while walking trails. Every state park has them and so do many city parks, which lead to little beauty spots and phases of city life which are, unfortunately, obscured and forgotten.

Several clubs around the country make life easier, and more economical, for the serious walker on the trail. In the East, the Appalachian Trail extends 2000 miles through 14 states, between Mount Katahdin, Maine, and Mount Oglethorpe, Georgia. It reaches its highest elevation, nearly 6000 feet, in the Great Smokies, its lowest a few feet above sea level at the Hudson River. Lakes are numerous along the northern portions; the South has more of the tumbling brooks and timbered ridges. The trail was developed and is kept cleared and marked through the efforts of a number of clubs, coordinated by the Appalachian Trail Conference. Overnight facilities vary, from such places as the celebrated Long Trail Lodge, at Sher-

The high walk: in the midst of tall timbers on the Oregon Skyline Trail, in view of the peaks of the Three Sisters, above timberline. Northwestern trails, relatively little trod, penetrate primitive mountain woodlands.

burne Pass, Vermont, to lean-tos. Generally the open shelters are free for anyone to use; closed shelters may be rented at 50¢ per person for members (minimum fee of $2 for non-members). The Appalachian Trail Conference, 1916 Sunderland Place, N.W., Washington, D.C., publishes a series of five guidebooks (average price, $3).

The West has higher mountains. Consult the Colorado Mountain Club, 400 Josephine Street, Denver, for hiking along the 14,000-foot Continental Divide; and these three groups in the Pacific States: the Sierra Club, 220 Bush Street, San Francisco, California; Mazamas Club, Pacific Building, Portland, Oregon, and Mountaineers Club, 523 Pike Street, Seattle, Washington.

Fishing, an ideal family vacation venture, keeps youngsters occupied and happy. Wise traveling parents plan rest stops where children can stretch their legs—and cast a line.

Trout for breakfast! Fresh-caught fish, a treat of outdoor cooking, saves money, too.

There is now under development the Pacific Crest Trail System, 2265 miles from the Canadian to the Mexican borders, but the principal sections presently open to use are the Washington Cascade Crest Trail, Oregon Skyline Trail, and the John Muir Trail in California. The northwestern trails penetrate a little-known, primitive America, unspoiled, refreshing, and invigorating. In time they will be photographed, well described, crossed, and recrossed. For the moment they are vestiges of the wilderness, punctuated with high mountain lakes, glaciers, and alpine meadows. The U. S. Forest Service has constructed trailside shelters along the way.

If hiking is too strenuous, then turn to fishing for your share of the outdoors. Carry a rod and reel whenever you travel and make the most of this relaxing, expense-low sport, a genuine vacation-type experience. Just be aware of local regulations and comply with them; it may cost money if you don't.

Share fishing sorties with your kids as a family venture. Speaking practically, you've got to keep the children happy or else you will have a perfectly miserable trip. Let them fish every chance you get, and, when you stop for an outdoor lunch, try to pick a spot near a stream or pond where they can drop a line. It will make their day—and add to yours. And don't forget that a fresh-caught fish provides one of the taste delights of outdoor cooking, to say nothing of the money you save.

Eating outdoors has always been a direct way to reduce vacation costs, but until recent years it was far too tedious and time-consuming for many people. Now, with a host of modern utensils and products, preparing a vacation meal is simple, streamlined, and painless.

Think of all you can do with canned goods, frozen and powdered foods, paper plates and containers, and that modern miracle, all-purpose aluminum foil. Canned food—fruits, juices, meats, and vegetables —packs easily and requires no refrigeration. You can stop at a supermarket along the way to pick up frozen foods; they come in a tremendous range which enables you to plan a simple, well-balanced, and inexpensive meal.

Then, instead of using pots and pans, you tear off a sheet of aluminum foil and cook your foods in it. Foil opens a multitude of outdoor culinary possibilities—and there is no scouring of pots to follow. As for cooking, it isn't even necessary to build a fire. In thirty seconds or so you can set up a one- or two-burner cook stove, light a match, and do your cooking with clean propane gas from disposable cylinders. At meal's end all you need is boiling water to add to your instant coffee and cream.

How much do you save eating outdoors? A family of four can have a meal for the same amount as one person, two at the most, in a restaurant. And with all credit to the creative art of interior decorating, the dining room has not yet been built to match the decor and atmosphere provided by a shade tree, a greensward, and a stream.

This is not to suggest that you prepare every vacation meal, or that you make a full-scale production of those you do. Without relieving Mother of household chores, including responsibility for the meals, a family vacation isn't quite right. So unless you are an avid outdoor cook, plan to eat simply. Even if you're on a camping trip, treat yourself to occasional restaurant service.

Roadside eating is wonderful for children in transit. In a restaurant they are unsettled; the food and atmosphere are different from those at home. In the time it takes to find a restaurant you would want to patronize, and then to wait to be served and to sit through the meal, you could well prepare your own fare. A further inducement is that outdoors the kids get a chance to romp and work off their energy. They absorb some of the local scenery and flavor, and you do too.

Highways are dotted with roadside parks, or waysides, equipped with tables, benches, safe drinking water, and often grills. Pennsylvania alone has 42 miniature roadside parks and 800 picnic tables along its highways and the Pennsylvania Turnpike. There is no need for cooking utensils or washing dishes, if you carry a supply of paper napkins, paper plates and cups, plastic or wooden knives, forks and spoons, and a thermos. You don't even need the thermos if you buy soft drinks and milk just before you stop to eat.

Oh yes, you can keep your foods cold in the latest aluminum innovation, a portable cooler made of laminated foil. It costs less than a dollar, and though it doesn't store ice, it works as well as the expensive, heavy metal coolers. This new magical gadget, named Stone's Stonewall Iceless Ice Box, is light as a feather.

Which goes to show how much easier life on the road has become since the Ice Age!

4

Lodgings, and How to Pick Them

Of all the money you spend away from home, about 60 per cent will be for food and lodgings. So these should be your principal targets for economy. However, it is just as important that you select the right kind of accommodations and enjoy your vacation meals—saving in itself cannot be enough. Curiously, despite the tremendous range in overnight facilities, many travelers are hesitant and unknowing. The result: they spend more than necessary and stay at places unsuited to their real desires and needs.

Following are the four principal types of lodgings, with suggestions on choosing the one that really suits your taste and purse:

Mother gets a break at the daily buffet luncheon served informally at the attractive Forest Hills Hotel, Franconia, New Hampshire. The children, meanwhile, are spending their time with a counselor.

1. The cabin or cottage, for the economy-minded family planning to spend a week or more at one place; particularly desirable with small children.

A cottage is the closest thing to being a home away from home. You feel relaxed with more than one room to move around in, and the youngsters are easier to handle. You don't have to dress them before each meal and you can prepare your own menu for them. Remember also that the more services you perform for yourself the less your vacation will cost. By staying in a cabin you do not have to pay restaurant prices for meals, nor do you have to tip for them. It is quite true that Mother will still have to cook, but at least she will be able to look out on a lake front or a mountainside. By using paper plates and cups she can reduce time spent in washing dishes, and for variety you can always dine out.

Cabins in national parks and forests and in state parks are among the most popular and consequently in great demand. Try to place your reservation early, but even if you are too late for this year, the effort will be worth it so you will be acquainted with procedures and facilities for next year.

Mom strums a ukulele in front of the family cabin at Letchworth State Park, New York. She still has to cook, but the surroundings are in her favor. Such accommodations are popular and demand early reservations.

For cottages at seasides and mountains, write to official state agencies and local chambers of commerce. They will furnish descriptive literature, including a directory of places to stay, complete with price range. Your friends and neighbors are the best source of information on accommodations; if they, with comparable taste, were pleased, the chances are that you will be too. Unless you have such recommendation, or know of the establishment by reputation, hesitate about placing a deposit before you see it yourself. It is quite true the owners must protect themselves from the unfair practice of cancellation without notice, but before you send any money through the mail you ought to be reasonably sure you have picked the right place.

2. The resort hotel, best if you measure your vacation in terms of leisure, service, and your wife's relief from kitchen chores. It costs more than cottage life, but there is little difference in expenses between the motel route (including meals, entertainment and attractions) and the resort hotel.

The modern motel often provides resort hotel facilities. The five-story Charterhouse, at Alexandria, Virginia, shown here, has swimming and wading pools, playground, recreation center, TV in every room, dining room and coffee shop.

Resort vacationing is wonderful for rest and relaxation. Often, areas of interest are at hand. At vacation's end, every member of the family, parents and children, comes away feeling he has been treated like a millionaire, and the expenditure may be no more than if they'd spent the time in touring.

To cite examples, a fine resort, the Forest Hills, Franconia, New Hampshire, surrounded by the White Mountains, provides golf, swimming, tennis, movies, bingo, clambakes, evening entertainment, and counselors to handle the children at least part of the time. The Bedford Springs Hotel in Pennsylvania's Allegheny Mountains enables youngsters to work off their energy at a supervised playground, pony ring, swimming pool, and private lake, while their parents are freed for golf, tennis, or evening dancing. The Elkhorn Lodge, Estes Park, Colorado, has a nine-hole putting green, Sunday guest rodeos, square dancing, and a complete junior program as part of its planned activities.

Weigh the effect on your wife's morale of a week at this type of resort hotel. She can dress up and look glamorous, be waited on hand and foot. She breakfasts in luxury, instead of in her own kitchen or at a roadside coffee shop. At resort hotels today, whether in New England or Florida, Virginia or California, luncheon is usually served al fresco at poolside, which means that it is not necessary to change at lunchtime.

The contemporary resort stresses service, informality, and atmosphere, with a cost of $325 and up per week for a family of four.

Check with your friends and neighbors on places they have stayed and liked. You can also consult a reputable travel agent for literature and reservations. For the most part, a travel agent's services are directed to booking tours, cruises and overseas travel, with no bearing at all on domestic motoring. However, agents are the appointed representatives of resort hotels, which pay them commission for booking reservations. In cases where a simple reservation is involved an agent should charge you no more than it costs to deal direct with the hotel (except for long distance calls or telegrams).

3. The modern motel, when you're on a touring vacation. You drive to your door, unpack at your leisure, without timidity or tipping, and that's it.

Or at least that is it at some motels. Others are larger and more sophisticated. Instead of parking at your door, you may be on the second or third floor. The facilities and services, swimming pool included, unquestionably provide added comfort and convenience—but you pay for them.

The motel field is booming, changing; at least 1,500 new motels are opening every year. The original type, a 15 or 20 unit place usually operated by husband and wife, is being obscured in the surge of 50, 100 and 200 unit motor hotels complete with resort facilities.

If you want to use that swimming pool and the added services, stop at one of the luxury-type motels. However, if your principal interest is in finding a clean, air-conditioned room with good beds and bath, a little search will lead to medium priced accommodations. Many people don't realize this because of the glamorous show made by the larger motels; motorists sometimes feel embarrassed about looking around for the less expensive places, though they needn't be. Just don't travel too long—the better grade reasonable rooms sell before 6 or 7 p.m. Be selective, not timid. You have every right to inspect your room before you accept it—if the manager refuses to show you the room, this is not the place for you.

How do you choose a motel for the night? From the outside look for these features:

· Attractive location in the community. You don't want your family in the wrong-end-of-town environment.

· A location back from the highway. Picture the place at midnight; will trucks roll by your window?

· Neat exterior and grounds; paved drive and adequate parking. If it's not well kept outside, the chances are not too bright for the interior.

· Restaurant nearby, if not at the motel.

· Approval sign of a reputable organization like the American Automobile Association or a motel group. Those affiliated with Quality Courts, though high priced, offer most in facilities and services. Master Hosts and Best Western are usually on the same price level as Quality. Congress of Motor Hotels, Superior and Courtesy Courts may be a shade lower. These are not chains, but promotional associations of motel operators, who conduct their own inspection—and can be their own severest critics! Most of the franchise operators (Howard Johnson, Congress Inn, Holiday Inn and TraveLodge) and the expanding chains (Marriott, Hotel Corporation of America's Charterhouses, Hilton, Sheraton, Knott) are members of the motel groups, too. The AAA maintains the most extensive coverage of all, with uniform national inspection standards.

If you're going to a crowded area during the peak of the season, plan your arrival carefully and try to make a reservation in advance. If you don't have time to write, try Western Union's new reservation service. It works this way: Western Union contacts the motel or hotel of your choice and if space is unavailable tries others in the same range. You pay for a round-trip telegram plus 50¢. If you don't have time to wait for confirmation, you call Western Union's "Reservation Desk" on arrival at your destination. The cost for this service is $1 plus the one-way telegram charge. Besides assuring you of a room, it saves you the trouble and cost of contacting one and possibly more establishments yourself.

4. Hotels in certain large cities offer a summer family vacation rate, including free parking. Pick one with a pool and you have a good value.

Otherwise, the large chain-type hotel is designed for conventioneers and expense account trade, and not for the budget-conscious family market. The less spectacular, lower priced hotels in the big cities are the ones interested in vacationers the year round.

Smaller city hotels, though losing ground to the motels, are sometimes a good value for people traveling without children. They may be fairly old but that in itself lends a certain warmth and atmosphere; many rooms are modernized and renovated, rates are modest and free parking often available. The bellboy, unlike his big city counterpart, appreciates a quarter tip.

Don't overlook the unique opportunity to stay at some of those rare smaller hotels or inns associated with history or literature. You will feel you are getting far more than a bed for the night staying at such places as: the Hathaway House, the converted old bakery on the grounds of the House of the Seven Gables, Salem, Massachusetts; the Lincoln House, in which Abraham Lincoln, Daniel Webster and Calvin Coolidge stayed in their times, and the Publick House, a restoration of a 1771 coaching tavern, both at Sturbridge, Massachusetts; the Treadway Maryland Inn, Annapolis, Maryland; and the Grand Imperial, fresh from the mining days of the '80's, Silverton, Colorado. There are more of these colorful places than you think. Keep your eye open for them as you travel.

Or consider this specific nomination for an all-around quality vacation at moderate cost: Callaway Gardens, at Pine Mountain, Georgia, a new beauty spot on the American scene. Here you can stay at a 50-unit Quality Court motel ($10 double), swim at a man-made sand beach, play golf at a fine nine-hole lakeside course, fish or boat in the lake. The food served at the dining room and outdoor pavilion is distinctly Southern, but whether you like Southern cooking or not, you will enjoy a meal here.

Callaway Gardens, 85 miles south of Atlanta on U. S. 27, was established by Cason Callaway, Georgia industrialist and philanthropist. There are 2500 acres of landscaped gardens, with scenic drives and a bird study trail. Admission is 75¢, children 35¢. For youngsters: miniature train ride, canoeing, paddleboats, water skiing.

A new touch in Georgia's hills—Robin Lake, with its man-made half-mile curving sand beach and pavilion, in one section of Callaway Gardens. The white sand is imported from the coast.

Eating places like the Pirate's House, in Trustees' Garden Village, Savannah, are located in vacation areas and along travel routes. This restaurant serves Savannah specialties in a setting that recalls an episode from Stevenson's Treasure Island.

5

The Price of a Good Meal

Good food at any price is not easy to find along America's vacation routes. For the most part the fare is either standard and expensive or the "greasy spoon" variety, possibly cheaper but loaded with trouble.

If you must choose between these two alternatives (there is a third, as we shall see presently), stick with the standard and safe. The first rule of vacation eating must be: avoid any place where sanitation or cleanliness is suspect. You cannot afford to gamble with food poisoning (often misnamed ptomaine), diarrhea and, worst of all, with dysentary, a chronic disease.

Until such time as all the states develop and enforce uniform, high standard restaurant regulations, you will do best, even at average eating places along the road, to keep away from mixed salads, custards, puddings, cream-filled pies. Such foods improperly covered or unrefrigerated are bacteria nesting grounds. You will be much safer by ordering hot, freshly cooked, or canned foods.

The third alternative is to start early in the morning with only juice or coffee, stop for a mid-morning brunch and then settle for fruit or a brief roadside picnic stop (see roadside rests in "Tenting on the New Campground") between then and dinner. In this way you avoid overeating and save enough on the travel budget for one really good meal a day.

Eating, good eating, should be part of the vacation experience, in the same sense as visiting a famous garden or historic objective. And, in the final analysis, the cost of a meal you will enjoy and care to remember need be no higher than that of a poor one.

It *is* worth the effort. Do not settle for your vacation meals as simply so many ounces of sustenance, or for an endless round of routine, standardized fare. Join the process of eating with the other elements of your trip; when you go into an area let dining—or even breakfasting—become an adventure in culinary ways and regional dishes. Look for those restaurants where you will not only find good food (the basic essential, after all) but the kind of surroundings and atmosphere in which to spend a useful, entertaining hour or more. Give your youngsters a break by seeking the places where they will have diversion, rather than just the ritual of another restaurant meal.

The taste of an epicure is not required to appreciate a good meal in pleasant surroundings. Avoid the tendency to confuse swank decor with quality food, for this only leads to unrewarding experiences at high prices.

Some meals very likely will cost more than you normally pay. On occasion, especially when they give you a vacation highlight, they are worth the difference. Here are four suggestions to help you on the road to better vacation eating:

· In your pretrip planning, consider some of the places you'll want to stop for a meal. Spot them on the map you travel by—just as you do the travel attractions in your itinerary. Ask friends if they have any recommendations, or buy one of the published guides to good eating.

· Determine to seek out the restaurants that specialize in local dishes. Don't go overboard for the same kind of food you can eat at a French, or pseudo-French, restaurant at home.

· Follow the truck drivers or ask service-station attendants? No, you are likely to end up eating pork chops served by their favorite waitress at a one-arm diner. Odds are that truck drivers do not stop at these same spots on their vacations. Ask local advice, yes, but from a motor-court operator, gift-shop owner, chamber of commerce.

· When in doubt about a roadside eating place, follow one restaurant man's advice: "Look for the local licensed cars. You can't fool the local people."

The ideal circumstance is when the meal, the setting, and the environs can be thought of as harmonious components of an entity. You will come close to the ideal at these famous eating places:

King's Arms Tavern, the finest of Colonial Williamsburg's several notable restaurants, as popular now as in the eighteenth century, when guests included William Byrd, George Washington, and Baron von Steuben (he liked it so well he ran up a $300 bill for lodging, board, and drinks). In one of its candlelit dining rooms, waiters in colonial dress serve you succulent English mutton chops with a tankard of ale, topped off with greengage ice cream. It is not inexpensive ($5–$7), but a rare experience, particularly when after dinner you stroll along Duke of Gloucester Street, its soft darkness punctuated by the glow of ancient street lamps. For lunch one day at Williamsburg stop at Chowning's Tavern, a reconstructed alehouse, for the hot Brunswick stew and pecan pie ($1.75); if it is a fair day, lunch under the grape arbor in the garden.

The Jordan Pond House, in Acadia National Park, Maine, near the park entrance at Seal Harbor, where you see Frenchman Bay's blue waters flowing into the Atlantic, the splashing breakers swirling high against rocky, granite cliffs. Have the charcoal-broiled Maine lobster, with popovers and then fruit ice cream ($3.50) on the Pond House porch or lawn. After lunch stroll the easy trail along Jordan Pond through the pine and hardwoods of a beautiful forestland.

The Pirate's House, in Savannah's Trustees' Garden Village, a choice century-old seafarer's inn filled with nautical curios. Try the sherry-flavored crab-meat stew and black-bottom pie ($2). Trustees' Garden, the pride of Savannah, was established by Oglethorpe, became in time a sailors' haunt and a blighted slum before its sparkling rehabilitation within the past decade.

La Placita, a lovely hacienda in Albuquerque's Old Town, a link with the storied Spanish past dating to 1706. A Mexican dinner, of

Good eating becomes a worth-while vacation experience, and costs no more, at Chowning's, a reconstructed eighteenth-century alehouse at Williamsburg.

course: sopa, enchilada, tacos, tortillas, arroz español, and for dessert the custard called natillas ($2.50). From the hacienda stroll the adjoining ancient patio, now lined with shops and art displays, and the Plaza, one of the first European settlements in the Southwest.

Knott's Berry Farm, near Disneyland, California, a treat especially for children. The place started as a simple berry farm 30 years ago, but during the depression the Knott family turned to serving meals and assembled a few western relics as an attraction. Now they can serve 1750 people at one time, can park 6000 cars. Their specialty, the chicken dinner ($2.25), is still served with homemade berry jam and berry pie and boysenberry sherbet offered as dessert. The collection of relics? It grew into an entire old-time community, complete with railroad, gold mine, ghost town, and wagon camp, good for hours of free entertainment.

Quality eating places are suggested as part of the "Fifteen Favorite Vacations" later in the book, and in connection with the state capitals in Chapter 7. Others you will enjoy:

Northeast (See also Tours 2, 3, 4)

Kennebunkport, Maine: the Olde Grist Mill. Turn off Maine Turnpike at Intersection 3, for Kennebunkport, art and literary colony, summer resort. Converted old mill with seafood a specialty.

Stowe, Vermont: The Lodge at Smugglers' Notch, near Mount Mansfield, the rooftop of the Green Mountains. The Notch, a forested gorge, was once a smugglers' hideout in conducting illicit trade with Canada. The Lodge ranks with the Nation's finest dining places. This area is beautiful, and less crowded, in autumn.

North Conway, New Hampshire: Eating House. Huge picture windows face the Skimobile, an ingenious tramway to the top of Cranmore Mountain. Carries skiers in winter, sight-seers in summer ($1.25; children, 75¢) to lofty summit overlooking 100 miles of White Mountain scenery.

Sturbridge, Massachusetts: Lincoln House. Dine in a historic mansion located, appropriately, at the gateway to Old Sturbridge Village, 200-acre re-creation of a typical early New England village. (Admission to area and all exhibition buildings, $2; youngsters under 17, $1; under 12, 60¢.) Luncheons also served during summer at village green tavern.

Princeton, New Jersey: Nassau Tavern and Princeton Inn, both distinguished dining rooms, linked with Princeton University's hallowed traditions. They are convenient to the campus, established two centuries ago, presided over early in this century by Woodrow Wilson.

Philadelphia, Pennsylvania: the two Bookbinders—The Old Original and Sea Food House; both old, reasonable, centrally located for sight-seeing to Independence Hall and other points.

Baltimore, Maryland: Miller Brothers, downtown; have Maryland crab (cakes, stew, fried, or boiled) or other sea food. Visit the Peale Museum's collection of prints, models, and paintings of clipper ships, and Fort McHenry National Monument, where Francis Scott Key saw the banner yet waving.

Southeast (See also Tours 5, 6, 7, 11)

Berkeley Springs, West Virginia: Park View Inn. Fine home cooking at an attractive small hotel adjacent to the state-operated mineral baths (try one!—refreshing, reasonably priced), one of the country's oldest spas, George Washington's favorite.

Fredericksburg, Virginia: General Washington Inn. Colonial-style dining room serving southern dishes. Convenient for sight-seeing Washington family homes and four key Civil War battlefields around Fredericksburg.

Shenandoah National Park, Virginia: Big Meadows Lodge, atop the

Skyline Drive, looking out at the Appalachian ranges and the Shen-andoah Valley meadows below.

Harrodsburg, Kentucky: Beaumont Inn. Epitome of the bluegrass country's traditions in good food, gracious living. Old Fort Harrod nearby commemorates first permanent English settlement west of the Alleghenies. Drive to the horse farms at Lexington.

Wilmington, North Carolina: Fergus Ark. Veritably an ark, a sea-food restaurant aboard a former river freighter on the Cape Fear River. Wilmington's best season: the Azalea Festival in late March.

Charleston, South Carolina: Perdita's, on Exchange Street, and the Rampart Room of the Fort Sumter Hotel. Both are at the colorful harbor, bordered with palmettos and live oak, facing Fort Sumter and the bay. Best time for Charleston: March, when the plantation gar-dens reach peak of bloom.

Tampa, Florida: Las Novedades. Features Cuban cooking, different than Spanish and Mexican. In Ybor City, Spanish quarter of grilled balconies, tiled roofs, and patios. Famous cigar factories welcome visitors Monday through Thursday.

Middle West (See also Tours 8, 9, 10)

Dearborn, Michigan: Dearborn Inn. Changed since Henry Ford built it and entertained in his way (early American dances; no liquor), a place of lively charm and automotive talk. Convenient to Henry Ford Museum and Greenfield Village (admission, 85¢; children under 15, 40¢; under 6, free) and the Ford Rotunda.

Nashville, Indiana: Colonial Restaurant. In the heart of the Brown County hills, surrounded by craft shops and art galleries; two miles from Brown County State Park.

Elgin, Illinois: the Milk Pail. At the Fin 'n Feather Farm, Route 25; most food you eat here is grown in the garden or the farm beyond.

Chicago, Illinois: the Berghoff. Heart of downtown, the type of ex-cellent old German restaurant constantly growing scarcer. Stockyard Inn, at the Union Stockyards. But don't let its location fool you; it is worthy of the meat packing tycoons whose paintings are on its walls. You pick your own steak for broiling.

Milwaukee, Wisconsin: Karl Ratzsch's. The spirit of Milwaukee, its German sauerbraten, schnitzel steaks, and collection of old glassware and steins.

Hayward, Wisconsin: Logging Camp Cook Shanty. Long tables, lumberjack style, one selection daily, but all you can eat for $2, chil-dren, $1. In Historyland Indian Village (admission, 50¢; children, 25¢), where the Chippewas demonstrate trapping, tanning, logging.

Homestead, Iowa: Bill Zuber's. Home-style German food, in the

Amana country, settled a century ago by a religious sect; these frugal people thrive on their community farming and manufacturing ventures. One Homestead dwelling is furnished in style of the early settlers.

Park Rapids, Minnesota: Rapid River Logging Camp. Replica of a lumber camp dining hall with all you can eat for $2, children $1. In the Mantrap-Belle Taine region, offering some of the country's finest lake fishing.

West (See also Tours 12, 13, 14, 15)

Colorado Springs, Colorado: Flying W Ranch. Chuck-wagon dinners served outdoors on a huge working ranch, Monday through Friday (Friday, rainbow trout). Visit the new Air Force Academy.

Cripple Creek, Colorado: Imperial Hotel. Continental buffet, top steaks and sea food. The Imperial, built in 1891, has been modernized, but entire decor and furnishings preserve the atmosphere of bonanza days. (Closed September through May.) Cripple Creek's summer feature: outstanding melodrama, in authentic surroundings.

Dallas, Texas: Arthur's Steak House. Western atmosphere and meat Texans are proud to ascribe to their domain. Dallas has many points of interest, including the Hall of State, Aquarium, Southern Methodist and Baylor universities.

Ketchum, Idaho: Warm Springs Ranch Inn, where you can catch your own dinner in the private trout pond. Ketchum is in Sun Valley's backyard, or vice versa.

Boise, Idaho: Gold Rush Room. Large size steaks; pork ribs smoked over applewood. Real gold, in various forms from the old Idaho boom cays, on display around the walls.

San Francisco, California: Fisherman's Grotto, Fisherman's Wharf, overlooking the Bay. Cathay, in the heart of the largest Chinese community outside China. Trader Vic's, expensive, but worth the price for atmosphere and good food.

Pismo Beach, California: Plessas Tavern. Home of the delectable baked pismo clam, of course.

San Diego, California: Manuel's. Mexican specialties served in historic building and garden patio, in San Diego's Old Town, the original Spanish settlement in California.

Seattle, Washington: Bush Garden Sukiyaki. Japanese atmosphere, Japanese food, complete with beer and sake. Crawford's Sea Grill; the view of oceangoing vessels and rising peaks across the Sound to accompany barbecued crab.

Snoqualmie, Washington: Snoqualmie Falls Lodge. In the mountain community of towering Douglas firs, snowy peaks, lakes, and 250-foot-high Snoqualmie Falls. Rise early and make it for Sunday farm breakfast (phone for reservations).

Tips on food and drink for infants:

Is your baby on fresh, pasteurized milk? Ask your doctor if you can rely on pasteurized milk purchased en route. If the baby is on formula, ask the physician about changing to dried or evaporated milk. If he approves, start several weeks early and try to complete the switch by departure time.

When you leave, carry a thermos of water from home so that infants (and smaller children) are not immediately subject to change in water. Start each day as you travel with a fresh supply from a safe source. The easiest way to provide the baby's water: sterilize bottles at night and fill with boiled water before sealing. If you're using evaporated milk, fill other bottles with the proper amount of boiled water; then at mealtimes add the correct amount of milk from a small can.

6

Everyman's Playground, the Public Lands

The highest mountain, the widest lake, the deepest forest, the finest of all scenery—these are found on public lands, those parcels of real estate we own in equal portions and are equally entitled to enjoy. Parks, forests, and reservoirs are in every corner, accessible at relatively little cost, offering pleasure and economy hand-in-hand.

The public lands are many. To know them, their differences in purpose and facilities, opens the door to endless vacation possibilities, and if you already are acquainted with some of them an even better trick is to locate the lesser publicized and uncongested, but no less attractive, areas. (See "Plan Now, Play Later" for sources of literature.)

Public lands in one sense are playgrounds. But they have a deeper meaning. They express the American spirit and heritage in many forms, disclosing to each individual his own picture of the past and future. The wonder is that so many years ago, when expansion and growth were the order of the day, these lands were set aside.

The most widely publicized and heavily visited of the public recreation areas are the national parks; so let's change the pace by considering first the national forests, 150 magnificent areas covering 180 million acres in 39 states and Puerto Rico. The national forests occupy one-tenth of the nation's land surface, one-fifth of the Western states.

Maroon Lake and the towering peaks of the Maroon Bells, in White River National Forest, a beauty spot of the Colorado Rockies, are near accommodations from campgrounds to dude ranches.

Many of the forests have been remote and inaccessible, but now they are coming into reach, opening a national treasure chest of scenic and recreational wonders.

The difference between the forests and parks? Though both exemplify conservation—planned, intelligent use of natural resources—there is a definite distinction between them. The national parks, administered by the Interior Department, have been set aside for public enjoyment as inviolate outdoor museums, preserved and protected. The national forests, administered by the Agriculture Department, in contrast, provide for "multi-purpose" use—timber harvesting, livestock grazing, mining, and hunting, which are not allowed in the national parks. The U. S. Forest Service was established in 1905, when Theodore Roosevelt was President, in order to protect and perpetuate forest lands through intelligent management and planning.

The beauty of the forests has been preserved for public enjoyment, and over the years recreation in the forests has grown tremendously in importance. Thousands of camping and picnic areas are easy to reach from many highways, and more are being developed. Of 140,000 road miles within, scarcely a mile is without some scenic attraction, while hiking and riding enthusiasts have 120,000 miles of trail to follow. The Appalachian Trail in the East extends through eight national forests, the Pacific Crest Trail System in the West through nineteen. Fishing, swimming, and boating are popular, too, with 70,000 miles of stream, thousands of ponds and lakes.

The economy-conscious vacationer has six different types of recreation areas to choose from in the national forests, as follows:

TYPE OF AREA	LOCATIONS	FACILITIES
High Mountain	Nine western states; over 8000 feet; cool days, cold nights.	Excellent hiking, riding, stream and lake fishing. Superb scenery, including glaciers. Most camps accessible by paved road, but some fine spots only by narrow mountain road or trail.
Mountain	Below 8000 feet; Black Hills of South Dakota; Ozarks of Missouri, Arkansas, Oklahoma, Appalachians of Virginia, West Virginia, North Carolina, Georgia, Tennessee; Alleghenies of Pennsylvania; White Mountains, New Hampshire; Green Mountains, Vermont. Warm days, cool nights.	Swimming, boating, fishing, riding. Resorts or small towns usually nearby. Some camps located on large reservoirs, lakes, rivers, or streams.
Lake	Along the Great Lakes, border lakes of Minnesota, large lakes of the West, such as Tahoe, Pend Oreille, Flathead; Shasta Reservoir, other reclamation and TVA reservoirs.	Swimming, sailing, boating, fishing.

TYPE OF AREA	LOCATIONS	FACILITIES
Wilderness	The wilderness areas of nine western states, border-lakes country of Minnesota. The 77 wilderness areas cover 14 million acres—last frontier in the United States.	Sacrifice comfort for natural solitude. Fishing, canoeing, camping.
Woodland	Missouri, Lake States, Ohio Valley, Piedmont region, Gulf Coast, Texas, Florida.	Camping, hiking, boating, fishing. Long season in the South, Florida camps open all year.
Charge Camps	Fifty forest campgrounds, mostly large, concessioner-operated. Well marked so campers looking for free facilities are not misled.	Special facilities, better than average cleanup. Charges vary from 25¢ per party to 25¢ per person per day.

Each individual forest has its own personality. These three, for example:

Ouachita National Forest, a million and a half acres in the highlands of Arkansas and Oklahoma, a beautiful area with the highest peaks in Arkansas, and 1500 miles of road leading to forest campgrounds, remote lakes, winding streams, game refuges and mountain towns like Mena and Pine Ridge. Ouachita, once the hunting ground of the Quapaw Indians, was discovered by the peripatetic Desoto. Large man-made lakes, like 50-mile long Ouachita, the newest, provide the full range of water sports. Ouachita became the first national forest east of the Great Plains (in 1907) and is the largest in the South. At the nearby resort city of Hot Springs every day is bath day; a million gallons of hot water pour daily from the mountain base to the tubs on Bathhouse Row. The water is favored therapy for a variety of ailments, but the "spa cure" is great to revitalize even the healthiest specimen. This is the only spa regulated by the Federal Government, the water source being within Hot Springs National Park. The Arlington Hotel ($12–$23 double) is an outstanding resort, but there are many lower priced accommodations.

The remote, roadless public lands, with clear streams and glacial peaks, are part of the vacation scene, too. Here a group of Trail Riders of the Wilderness look across snow-bordered Elbow Lake at 11,000 feet in Bridger Primitive Area, Wyoming. The author is at right.

White River National Forest, on Colorado's western slope, containing spectacular canyons, falls, mineral hot springs, and alpine lakes. Aspen, the recreation and cultural center, is within the forest, ringed by towering 14,000-foot peaks. Hiking and riding trails lead through aspen and spruce forests and high meadows. Overnight facilities range from improved camping areas to commercial cabins ($7–$12 double) and dude ranches ($150–$200 a week, American plan; children, half price). One of the most beautiful areas lies beside Maroon Lake at the foot of the majestic peaks, the Maroon Bells.

Bridger National Forest, Wyoming, the heart of the dramatic, history-rich Wind River Range, explored by Fremont, Kit Carson, Jim Bridger. One part of the Forest, Bridger Primitive Area, 383,000 acres of roadless country, embraces the headwaters of the Green River and mountain peaks up to 13,785 feet in elevation. Most accessible point by car is the newly expanded Elkheart Park campground, outside Pinedale, Wyoming (Route 187, southeast of Grand Teton and Yellowstone National Parks). From here you can hike or ride to any of

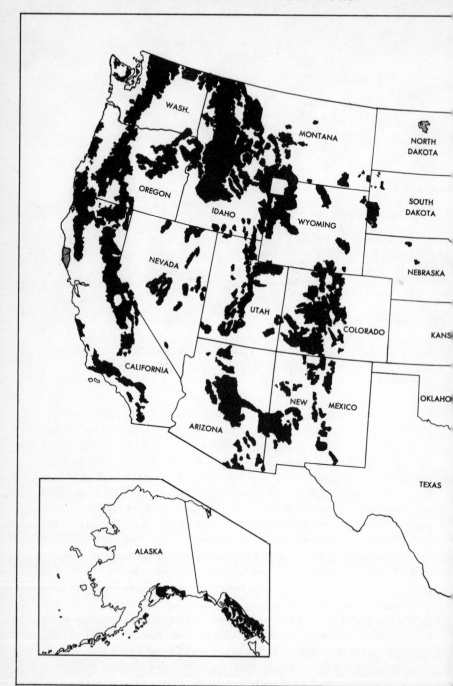

The Public Vacationlands

NATIONAL FORESTS

a thousand clear lakes, see elk, deer, antelope and moose, massive granitic boulders above timberline, Alpine wildflowers in bloom.

One way to explore the Bridger Primitive country (as well as several other wilderness areas administered by the Forest Service) is to join the Trail Riders of the Wilderness, guided summer groups which spend ten days to two weeks in camping on the trail. Prices range from $210 to $250, including full days of riding (except for time out for hiking, fishing), followed by evening campfires. For information, write the American Forestry Association, 919 17th Street, N.W., Washington, D.C.

Use of the national forests has zoomed. Unfortunately, overcrowding is a critical problem and many campgrounds carry 50 per cent above capacity. Your best solution is to visit the national forests during the week, rather than the weekend, if you can.

There is something else you can do: the forests deserve the interest of those who use them. Write your congressman and ask him for information on "Operation Outdoors," the Forest Service five-year program to modernize and expand its recreational facilities. "Operation Outdoors" merits the support of all Americans. It is sorely needed for the well-being of treasured woodland resources, as well as to provide elbow room for a recreation-conscious people.

Now for the national park system. Parks are not a new, nor even an American, creation. They were known in ancient civilization and were recognized as a mark of advancement in the development of European countries. In the settlement of the New World, open squares and commons were developed for community purposes. As cities grew, the city park system emerged with the establishment of Central Park in New York City in 1857. Seven years later, across the continent, Californians created the first state park in Yosemite Valley. And in 1870 a group of explorers around a campfire in Yellowstone agreed that instead of claiming this vast frontierland for themselves they would share it "as a public park or pleasuring ground for the benefit and enjoyment of the people." Thus the first national park came into being. Later (1916), the National Park Service was established by Congress to conserve the scenery, wildlife, and historic objects in the national parks, while providing for public use in such a way as to leave them "unimpaired for the enjoyment of future generations."

The National Park Service now administers some 25 million acres of land. Its 180-odd areas are divided in a variety of categories: parks, historical parks, monuments, military parks, memorial parks, battlefield parks, battlefield sites, historic sites, memorials, cemeteries, parkways, recreation areas, and a seashore recreation area. The difference, probably once purposeful, tends to be confusing now. In theory the 30 national parks are the most outstanding of all, but many of the other areas are equally significant with as much to offer. The point is made because a great many people limit their field, heading only for the "major" national parks while they overlook the values in the monuments and other areas.

The parks offer camping, hiking, fishing (no hunting); horseback riding for an hour or two on gentle trails or for days on end in wild, backwood country; in the winter, tobogganing, skiing, and snowshoeing. The park areas cover the sweep of nature, the seashore, desert, stark erosion of a million years, forest land, peaks high above timberline, timeless glaciers in motion. Birds and animals live free and untamed. The historical parks, monuments, and battlefields chronicle man's history, from his cliff-dwelling days down through the earliest western colonization, Revolution, and Civil War to the mechanical turn of our century.

Camping offers one of the most enjoyable ways, and certainly the most inexpensive, to explore the parks. But there are others too: between the wilderness site and the luxury hotel, accommodations include cabins and motel-type units. All these are privately operated under government concession and regulations. By and large, the rates are comparable to those outside the parks. At a number of areas, where nearby communities are not too far from principal points of interest, overnight facilities are provided entirely by private operators outside park boundaries.

The national parks have undergone an amazing revolution in use, if not in concept. Once they were mostly remote, western areas. The only sensible way to reach them was by rail, and it was a real adventure. Now a place like Yellowstone receives as many visitors in a week as during an entire summer 30 or so years ago. Today the park system is truly national, and even extends to Alaska, Hawaii, Puerto Rico, and the Virgin Islands. Providing millions of visitors with the means of enjoying and appreciating their parks, while preserving the land from misuse, is no small challenge to the National Park Service. Through the 10-year program, "Mission 66," the Park Service is presently undertaking an expansion of facilities scheduled for completion by its fiftieth anniversary in 1966. New roads and campgrounds are among the most apparent needs, but there are many others. As part of Mission 66, visitor centers, audio-visual materials, markers, and exhibits are providing modern, comprehensive explanation and interpretation of park features. And much-needed housing is being provided for park personnel and their families.

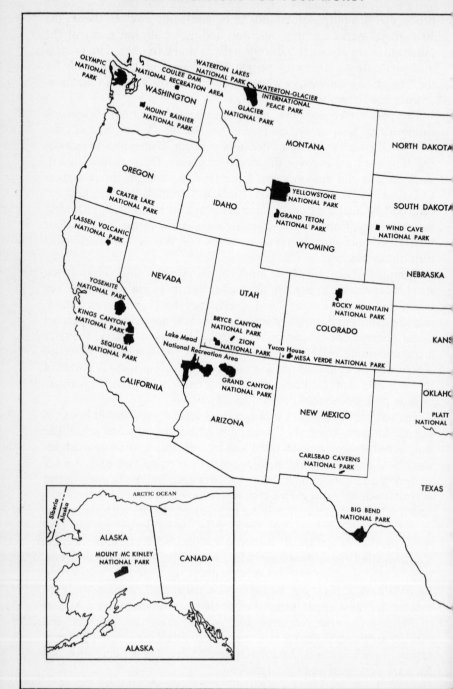

The Public Vacationlands

NATIONAL PARKS

ISLE ROYALE NATIONAL PARK

ACADIA NATIONAL PARK

SHENANDOAH NATIONAL PARK

MAMMOTH CAVE NATIONAL PARK

CAPE HATTERAS NATIONAL SEASHORE

GREAT SMOKY MOUNTAINS NATIONAL PARK

HOT SPRINGS NATIONAL PARK

EVERGLADES NATIONAL PARK

HAWAII NATIONAL PARK

THE HAWAIIAN ISLANDS

Roads are ending the isolation of Canyon de Chelly, Arizona, in the heart of the southwestern Indian country.

The new Pinnacles Terrace, at the Tennessee-Kentucky-Virginia boundary, high above Cumberland Gap, the historic link in the Wilderness Trail, through which early settlers streamed westward.

Mission 66, together with the national highway program, will bring relatively little-known areas within practical reach. New names are going to take their places alongside traditional park attractions. Some are well on the way now, and if you're the kind looking for the less crowded and the less publicized, consider some of these:

Cumberland Gap National Historical Park, 20,000 acres of mountain and valley at the boundary shared by Kentucky, Tennessee, and Virginia. The Gap was an important link on the Wilderness Road to Kentucky and the West, through which Daniel Boone, George Rogers Clark, and other early trail blazers guided 200,000 pioneer settlers between 1775 and 1796. The scenic overlook, 1000 feet high, provides a vantage above the Gap, while mountaintop hiking trails lead to the scenes of Civil War battles. Motel lodgings, Middlesboro, Kentucky, $6–$10 double.

Cape Hatteras National Seashore Recreation Area, the slender barrier islands off the North Carolina coast, preserving almost all that remains of the Atlantic beach front not commercially developed. Connecting bridges make this unusual park accessible from the mainland on the north, while a road, with ferry links, runs its full length from Nags Head through Ocracoke Island. A new ferry is due to open from Ocracoke to the mainland on the southern end. The Outer Banks, with their sand dunes, lonely villages, and Hatteras lighthouse, wore the aura of mystery for years. But now they are a splendid vacation area, affording fishing, swimming, sight-seeing, and camping on the beach. Summer mosquitoes can be a problem, so bring plenty of repellant. Autumn is a beautiful, quiet time and winter is generally mild (though much too cool for swimming, of course). Two nearby national monu-

The most unusual museum in the world—the new visitor center at Dinosaur National Monument, Utah-Colorado. The far wall is a cliffside, with dino-saur bones visibly embedded, as they have been for centuries.

ments are: Fort Raleigh, Manteo, site of the first British settlement, the "Lost Colony," and the Wright Brothers Memorial, Kitty Hawk, where the air age was born with that dramatic flight of 1903. The Carolinian Hotel at Nags Head ($20–$26 double with meals) is open all year and features excellent meals and supervised children's activities. Overnight facilities are also available in other villages. Boat charter, $30–$90 daily.

Dinosaur National Monument, near Vernal, Utah, 200 miles east of Salt Lake City, a vast wilderness of nearly 330 square miles, recently identified by violent controversy over the unsuccessful proposal to build a dam and flood a large part of it. Within its boundaries is the nation's richest deposit of dinosaur fossils. There is nothing in the world comparable to the new visitor center—one wall a cliffside with dinosaur bones embedded as they have been for millions of years. The principal scenic features are the deep, narrow canyons formed by the Green and Yampa Rivers; in 1959 a new road opened to Harpers Corner, 5000 feet above the confluence of the two rivers. Even more thrilling are boat trips operated on the rivers. Hotel, motel accommodations, Vernal, Utah, $6–$10 double.

Canyon de Chelly National Monument, 80,000 awesome acres of red cliffs and mysterious caves in eastern Arizona. After an eternity of isolation, modern roads are finally opening the heart of the Indian country. Prehistoric ruins along the canyon walls are among the finest in the Southwest. The Navahos have lived in the canyons for 200 years, not all of them peaceful. In one period they warred with the neighboring Pueblo Indians; in another they were massacred by the Spaniards in Canyon del Muerto, and in the 1880s Kit Carson and the cavalry tried to transplant them elsewhere. It didn't work, and the Navaho farmers are as much a part of the scene as the towering monoliths and canyon walls. Caution: Rim Road Drive in good condition, but motoring on canyon floor sometimes hazardous. Contact Thunderbird Guest Ranch, facing park headquarters, to rent special vehicle equipped for canyon driving ($20 for car and driver for half-day trip, up to four passengers). Accommodations, Thunderbird Guest Ranch, $9.50 double.

Water projects—those amazing dams and reservoirs that have reshaped twentieth-century America—have created new recreation facilities where none existed before. True, they were designed for other missions. The Tennessee Valley Authority has brought power to the Southland, the Bureau of Reclamation turned the western desert into a garden, and the Corps of Engineers brought floodwaters under control. But who, a generation ago, could have envisioned a vast water playground like Lake Mead rising out of the dry, empty spaces of Arizona and Nevada? Now there are four major recreation developments on the lake. Facilities include the Lodge at Boulder Bay ($7–$10 double), cabins at Overton Beach and Temple Bar ($4–$8), campgrounds (free), swimming beaches, diving floats, and picnic grounds.

Yet Lake Mead is only one of 140 reservoir recreational areas developed by the Reclamation Bureau and enjoyed by millions of boaters, fishermen, swimmers, and campers. Mead and several others of national significance have been transferred to the National Park Service; areas in the national forests are usually transferred to the Forest Service, and other areas are made available to state and local government agencies.

Guided tours are conducted (adults, 30¢; children under 12, free) at such great power plants as Hoover Dam, on the Boulder Canyon project in Arizona and Nevada; Shasta Dam, on the Central Valley project in California; Hungry Horse Dam in Montana, and Grand Coulee Dam on the Columbia Basin project in Washington. Visitors at Grand Coulee find something new, added in 1958: $200,000 worth of floodlights illuminating the world's biggest spillway in five changing colors. The huge concrete structure is already Washington State's best tourist attraction but the new splash of light makes it even more fascinating.

Visitors are also welcome at the dams of the TVA (admission, free), whose chain of 20-odd lakes extends through Alabama, Georgia, Kentucky, Mississippi, North Carolina, Tennessee, and Virginia. A decade ago these lakes were the object of seven million visits; the total now is more than 30 million. The most popular lakes: Kentucky, Guntersville, Wheeler, Norris, and Chickamauga. State parks and privately operated resorts in the TVA area provide accommodations ranging from fishing cabins and campgrounds to first-class motel units and hotels capable of housing 9000 visitors.

Norris Dam, Tennessee, first in the TVA system, was completed in 1936. Norris Lake, the reservoir formed by the dam, is bordered by an 800-mile shoreline, three state parks, fishing and resort centers. At another TVA development, on the Tennessee River near Knoxville, a place well suited for family vacationers is Watts Bar Village ($8–$12 double, also weekly rates) with one- to three-room housekeeping cottages; swimming and wading pools, playground, sailboats, and fishing.

Now meet the National Wildlife Refuges, 275 areas covering 17 million acres of land, which are just now attaining a place alongside parks and forests in our recreation patterns. With population ever rising and outdoor space diminishing, the opportunity to observe and photograph birds and animals in their natural surroundings is certain to be more welcome.

Happily, the wildlife refuges are not "locked up." Their primary mission is the protection and preservation of wildlife, but their secondary purpose is to provide for public enjoyment. Half the eight million visitors a year are interested in hunting and fishing, but the remainder come to picnic, swim, and enjoy uncluttered natural scenery. Many of the areas are easily reached from principal motor routes.

Theodore Roosevelt created the national wildlife refuges in 1903 to conserve animals, birds, and waterfowl from apparent inevitable annihilation in the rush of civilization across the land. His judgment has been well proven since; native wildlife coexists with humankind and the refuges have achieved rare success in rescuing many species from extinction. They have, for example, saved the trumpeter swan and are trying to save the whooping crane; they have helped preserve big animals of the western plains and mountains, the pronghorn antelope, bighorn sheep, buffalo, and the Texas longhorn, the old-time breed that once trod the Chisholm Trail.

These areas indicate the scope of the wildlife refuges:

· *Mattamuskeet, Pea Island, and Swanquarter,* on the North Carolina coast, include about 50,000 acres of land that furnish winter food and shelter for more than 100,000 waterfowl—one of the largest congregations of Canada geese on the Atlantic seaboard and more whistling swans than the average person is likely to see in a lifetime. Ducks, geese, and swans, which in summer scatter across the northern rim of the world from Labrador to Alaska, come down the skylanes in the fall; here, along a narrow Atlantic coastal strip, they find conditions for winter survival. Mattamuskeet, one of the few refuges with overnight facilities, has a modern, comfortable lodge accommodating 40 persons.

· *Okefenokee,* in southern Georgia, near U. S. 1, is one of the most primitive swamps in America. In its nearly 700 square miles of shallow water and hammocks of land are bear, deer, wildcat, raccoon, possum, otter, and alligator, that indomitable fellow called Pogo, along with Florida cranes and other birds. Once these were almost slaughtered into extinction by hunters and trappers. Boat trips into the trackless swamp are permitted only with a licensed guide, but a typical cross section may be seen at Swamp Park (admission, $1.25; children 6–12, 55¢) at the northern end. Modern accommodations and good food are available at nearby Waycross ($6–$12 double).

Entry to Pogoland! The start of the boat ride into Okefenokee Swamp Park, at the edge of the 700-square mile national wildlife refuge, the largest fresh-water swamp in America.

· The whooping crane, that almost vanishing breed, is protected at *Aransas Refuge,* on a broad peninsula near Corpus Christi, Texas, overlooking Matagorda Island and the Gulf of Mexico. Arriving in October from their recently discovered nesting ground on Great Slave Lake in Canada, they remain at Aransas until the end of March. An observation tower gives visitors a vantage point to watch the slender flock (less than 40) of these stately white birds. The 47,000-acre refuge is visited by nearly 300 other species—vast throngs of ducks and geese, sometimes more than 150,000 of them, ibises, egrets, and herons. Accommodations at Padre Island and Corpus Christi (double $6–$16).

· *Wichita Mountain Wildlife Refuge,* in southwestern Oklahoma, contains one of the largest herds of buffalo, as well as elk, deer, and once nearly extinct longhorn cattle. The 60,000-acre preserve looks largely as it did when the Cheyenne hunted here, but along with caring for wildlife it provides for camping, swimming, hiking, and other recreation. Hotel, motel accommodations in Lawton, $5–$8 double.

· The largest preserve in the United States, *Desert Game Range,* is at the back door to Las Vegas. It covers two million acres; its principal inhabitants, desert bighorn sheep, live in a rugged wilderness, ranging from desert to 12,000-foot mountains. Roads are few and unimproved, but visitors are increasing at the Corn Creek field station, 26 miles from Las Vegas, and other accessible parts of the refuge. A horse trail leads into the Red Rock area of the Spring Range.

State parks vary in size from the 2.2 million acres of New York's Adirondack Preserve to a small shrine of less than a city block. They complement the national park system, and you are likely to enjoy camping or fishing or hiking in one as much as the other. The scenic and historic values in some state parks are of the first magnitude; for example, the Niagara Reservation, New York; redwoods state parks in California; Valley Forge, where Washington wintered in Pennsylvania, and New Salem, Illinois, where Lincoln found his course in life. Jones Beach on Long Island, the most heavily used state park, accommodates 15,000 cars at one time.

William Randolph Hearst once reigned at San Simeon, California, while a group with names like Rockefeller, Morgan, and Harriman sojourned at Jekyll Island, Georgia. The private playgrounds of these gentlemen have since passed into other hands—they are among the 2000 state parks which offer to all the luxury of forest, mountain, lake, and seashore.

Oregon and California have the greatest number of state parks, 156 and 143 respectively. They are followed by New York, 127; Ohio, 113; and Washington, 110. On a given night all the state parks could, and sometimes do, sleep 200,000 persons—in cabins, lodges, hotels, tents and trailer camp sites, and organized camps. Camping has been largely a pursuit in the northern tier of states, but the southern states (notably Florida) are beginning to catch up.

The five states with the largest capacity in their hotels and lodges are Indiana, Oklahoma, Kentucky, South Dakota, and New York. Don't sell these facilities short, either. The new Western Hills Lodge in Sequoyah State Park is the showplace of Oklahoma; new lodges in Kentucky, Tennessee, and West Virginia are also among the best accommodations in those states.

State parks have been with us for a long time, but their greatest day lies ahead. As individual areas, each with its distinct appeal, they are emerging on the national travel scene. Reservoirs have been a tremen-

The Public Vacationlands

NATIONAL WILDLIFE REFUGES

dous stimulant to state park development through the Missouri River basin of the Midwest and in the TVA area of the South.

Here is a sample of outstanding state parks:

Franconia Notch, New Hampshire, the celebrated mountain gap in the White Mountains, with such prominent features as the Profile, Great Stone Face, and the Flume Gorge (admission, 50¢; children, 25¢; bus to foot of gorge, 20¢). The Lafayette Campground provides 50 tent sites, each with fireplace, table, and car parking space; the recreation building is equipped with showers and laundry equipment. Hardly a New England resort has a more unusual setting than Echo Lake, with mountains on three sides, where park visitors fish, swim, and boat.

Caledonia State Park, Pennsylvania, 1400 acres near Chambersburg, a scenic area containing the remains of an old charcoal furnace built in 1837 by Thaddeus Stevens, the southerners' hairshirt, and partially destroyed in 1863 by Jubal Early's rebel troops. Along with fishing, camping, and picnicking, facilities at Caledonia include a swimming pool and golf course. The historic Graeffenburg Inn ($5–$10 double) is an enjoyable park stop.

Spring Mill State Park, Indiana, near Mitchell, distinguished both by its scenery and too little publicized historic restoration, the Spring Mill village. The moss-covered ruins of this frontier trading post were discovered in a secluded hollow entirely surrounded by towering cliffs. It includes the original water-powered gristmill, reconstructed sawmill, post office, stillhouse, boot shop, apothecary, and lime kiln. The park contains about 100 acres of virgin timber, large specimens of white oak and yellow poplar; unusual caverns, underground streams with species of rare fish. A 40-acre lake provides swimming, boating, and fishing, and there are camping and picnic areas. Spring Mill Inn, one of the newest and best state park inns, is open all year ($15 double, American plan).

Cumberland Falls State Park, Kentucky, west of Corbin. The park's outstanding feature, Cumberland Falls, drops 65 feet, and on bright moonlit nights a moon bow can be seen in its mist. (The only other known moon bow is in South Africa.) Facilities cover a wide range, from camping to the famous DuPont Lodge ($5–$9 double).

Petit Jean State Park, Arkansas, near Morrilton, 65 miles from Little Rock. Park visitors share Petit Jean Mountain with Winthrop Rockefeller, whose Winrock Farm is adjacent and partly open to visitors. And well worth visiting, not only to see a rich man's place, but for the wonders he has worked in modern farming. The 4100-acre state park has fine features: Stephen Mather Lodge ($6–$9 double), housekeeping cabins, campgrounds, bridle paths, mountain scenery, fishing, and boating at Lake Bailey.

Longfellow-Evangeline State Park, Louisiana, on the banks of the beautiful, winding Bayou Teche, in the heart of the "cajun country," where many Acadians settled after being driven from Nova Scotia in 1765. At the Acadian House guides recount the story of Evangeline and Gabriel, the basis of Longfellow's famous poem; the historic house, built of hand-hewn cypress timbers fastened with wooden pegs, has been restored and furnished. Campgrounds are in the park nearby. The Park Lodge, a restaurant, specializes in Louisiana French food; and worth while, authentic souvenirs are sold at the Craft Shop, operated by Louisiana State University in order to perpetuate weaving, palmetto work, and basketry.

Itasca State Park, Minnesota, 28 miles north of Park Rapids, covering 32,000 acres, much of it water, including Lake Itasca, the source of the Mississippi River, which here begins its winding course to the Gulf of Mexico. The Itasca forest is dominated by stands of spruce and white pine, but contains nearly every kind of tree, plant, and wild animal native to Minnesota. There are daily launch excursions on Lake Itasca. Campgrounds, housekeeping cabins, and hotel accommodations at Douglas Lodge ($4–$7 double), which overlooks the lake, are available.

Custer State Park, South Dakota, five miles east of Custer, in the heart of the Black Hills, a 58,000-acre sanctuary for one of the world's largest buffalo herds, as well as deer, elk, bighorn sheep. Other noted features are the park zoo, housing many animals and birds, and the museum with displays on history, geology, and forestry. Hundreds of miles of trout stream flow through the park; the visitor can ride and hike through the Black Hills, swim and boat on beautiful lakes. There are four cabin and lodge areas, the best known being the Game Lodge ($5.50–$8 double), once the summer headquarters of President Calvin Coolidge. All the dining rooms in Custer State Park serve buffalo, elk, and trout. The chefs are happy to prepare your own catch of fish.

Once you arrive in a public park or recreation area, whether you plan to spend an hour, a day or week, begin with a call at the headquarters or visitors' center. Introduce yourself to the ranger, naturalist, or historian on duty. These men are dedicated to helping you get the most out of your stay. No question goes unanswered. Many of them are experts in their fields, but they are equally at home in conversation with children as with scholars.

Take advantage of the free programs. Not because they give you

A visit with the ranger at the Dickey Ridge visitor center starts this family off right for their tour of Shenandoah National Park, Virginia.

something to do at no cost, but because they will deepen your understanding and appreciation of the area. The National Park Service offers thousands of evening programs. At Yellowstone alone five separate evening programs are given every night during the summer (at Mammoth Hot Springs, Old Faithful, Fishing Bridge, Canyon, and the Thumb). At Mesa Verde visitors gather round the campfire on the mesa while the naturalist, with the valley and cliffs behind him, talks of an early American people and their civilization.

In visiting a national forest, stop at the nearest forest supervisor, ranger, or guard headquarters for firsthand information and local maps. The ranger knows the area and can help you avoid confusion. The same is true at the wildlife refuges, about 110 of which have full-time managers. It is advisable to write the manager, telling him your arrival date, number in your party, and your particular field of interest. This enables him to plan your trip over the refuge to best advantage. When you arrive, particularly if you did not have time to write in advance, call at refuge headquarters; you'll get suggestions for wildlife observations, photographic and recreation possibilities.

A word about conservation. Earlier in history it required only a score of well-placed, forward-looking citizens, such as Theodore Roosevelt, Gifford Pinchot and Stephen Mather, to safeguard the lands, waters, wildlife, minerals, and other natural resources. Now, in the era of heightened use and shrinking space, it is everyone's challenge.

Did you know there is scarcely a stream in the country where you can drink in certainty of pure water? Neither water nor land, which form today's playground treasures, can be taken for granted tomorrow. The best means to insure the continuing enjoyment of recreational resources is through public interest and support of constructive conservation measures. You will find your congressmen, governor, and state legislators are all aware of, and many are active in, this field. Find out what they are doing and give them encouragement, if you approve.

7

On Tour,
American Landmarks

"I spent a month in Europe," a traveler reported, "and I really took the tour! It cost a fortune, but it was worth it." Of course it was worth it—but as he ticked off the names of places he had visited his listener thought, Why, he hasn't seen many of the same kind of places in his own country. Nor would he consider them, even if he drove right by.

Foreign travel is a choice experience, but we too have beautiful colleges, churches, art galleries, government buildings, perhaps not as old, but at least our own, and that should count for something. To seek out noble landmarks an ocean or more away is a splendid thing to do, but why overlook America's? Seasoned travelers are able to locate without difficulty any number of points of interest that are inexpensive, that reflect some facet of Americana and are fun to visit.

State capitals are an example. If Washington, D.C., is so thoroughly attractive, why not these other seats of government spread across America? Each tells a story, in its art and architecture, its legislative chambers and governor's office, where great figures in history advanced their careers. Capital cities have an aura of their own, enlivened by political talk in restaurants, hotel lobbies, and capitol corridors. And at the favored eating spots you are likely to sample good food along with local atmosphere.

Every state capitol contains something of interest. Nevada's in Carson City, the smallest, sits atop a silver mine, and you can see a mining display underground. Oklahoma's, at Oklahoma City, has working oil wells on its grounds. The largest? At Austin, Texas, of course. State capitols come in all sizes and shapes, as new as our modern age and as old as colonial times.

For antiquity, Boston is probably our closest approach to the European. The Old State House was built in 1713 and reconstructed in 1747 while the "new" State House has been in continuous use since 1796—and that's a lot of Cabots, Lodges, and Curleys ago. Downtown, arrows mark the "Freedom Trail," a walking tour through winding streets, past old churchyards and burial yards, to points of interest like the North Church and Faneuil Hall. Durgin-Park, an eating place in the old market section, serves fine New England food reasonably priced. The traditions and personality of Boston are in its suburbs too—Cambridge, Lexington, Concord, and Quincy.

Massachusetts, however, yields to Maryland for the oldest state capitol still in daily use. The State House at Annapolis was completed in 1774, well in advance of its short term as capitol of the United States. A guide greets visitors and escorts them through the building, to such highlights as the old Senate Chamber, where Washington resigned his commission as commander in chief of the Continental Army, and to the office of the present governor. Annapolis, though best identified with the U. S. Naval Academy, is also notable for examples of Georgian architecture and for St. John's College, founded in 1696 as King William's School. The Cruise Inn, across the street from the capitol, is a popular, moderately priced dining place.

Virginia's capitol is probably the only one designed by a President. Thomas Jefferson, that able architect, created this handsome building with the typical Jeffersonian dome. Other places have copies of Houdon's statue of Washington, but the original is in the rotunda here. Richmond reeks with history about as much as Yankee Boston—dating back to the days of William Byrd and Patrick Henry's defiant speech at St. John's Church. In the old House of Delegates, Aaron Burr was tried for treason in 1807, Robert E. Lee accepted command

The oldest state capitol still in use, at Annapolis, Maryland. Free guided tours show the chambers used by Congress during its brief period as capital of the United States.

of the Virginia troops, and the Confederate Congress met from 1862 until its end. The Raleigh Hotel on Main Street has changed its name since it was Rueger's and the elite stopping place of Richmond, but it is still tops for its steaks and sea food.

The tallest state capitol, 34 stories high, is at Baton Rouge, a city that has weathered stormy history from the French and Spanish periods down through Huey P. Long. That flamboyant politician built the capitol in 1932, was assassinated in it three years later, and is entombed at the main entrance. Its observation tower, 27 stories up, overlooks the Louisiana scene of bayous and lakes. Baton Rouge is also home of Louisiana State University, where the Museum of Natural Science, and particularly its Gallery of Louisiana Birds, is an interesting new point to visit in the South.

Denver probably has the most handsome location of any capital, facing the snowy Rocky Mountains, and would be a great city to visit in any event. Coloradans constructed their capitol building as a showpiece, fashioned of granite walls, onyx pillars, and a dome of lead covered with gold—all native minerals. Denver has many fine attractions that are free, including the U. S. Mint and the network of municipally-owned mountain parks extending into the Rockies. Be sure to have one meal at the El Rancho, 18 miles west on U. S. 40, another at the Buckhorn Exchange. El Rancho, with a magnificent hilltop view of the Continental Divide, specializes in roast prime rib and steaks. Its unique lounge and bar, the Forge, is built around a huge, open-center fireplace, drinks served in containers shaped like blacksmith forges. The Buckhorn, too, features steaks and roasts, with a fantastic atmosphere—hundreds of antique guns and mounted wild animal trophies.

For a small city (population less than 30,000), Santa Fe exudes history and atmosphere. The Spaniards established a seat of government in 1609 when they built the Palace of Governors. This venerable structure later served as state capitol until 1909 and is still the primary attraction. Even in its newer buildings, through use of adobe and Pueblo architecture, Santa Fe preserves the feeling of its past. It is a blending of backgrounds, the Indian, Spanish, Mexican, American West, with a touch of modern easterners gone western. As an art center, Santa Fe encompasses everything from ancient Indian to latter-day abstractionism. The La Fonda Hotel ($9–$15 double) has become

The tallest state capitol, at Baton Rouge, Louisiana. Huey Long built it, then was assassinated here. The observation tower, on the twenty-seventh floor, overlooks landscaped grounds and the Louisiana countryside of lakes and bayous.

a landmark on the Plaza, while the Pink Adobe, a dining spot around the corner, is unusual, even in Santa Fe.

Helena's Last Chance Gulch has been renamed Main Street, but many of those curiously ornamented old mining camp buildings are still standing. They date back to the great gold rush of the 1860s, when four desperate prospectors struck pay dirt on their "last chance." Many state capitols are decorated with murals, but Montana's capitol is the only one with a mural by Charles Russell (Lewis and Clark meeting the Indians), the uncanny cowboy who learned art on the range. Drive out for a meal at the Frontier Town Dining Room, serving western food in a setting facing the Continental Divide and McDonald Pass.

On a high bluff, the Washington State Capitol at Olympia overlooks Puget Sound; visible in the distance are the snow peaks of Mount Olympus and Mount Rainier. The Legislative Building, most prominent of the capitol group, appears outstanding from the outside, with its huge dome, and proves equally interesting within. Other points worth touring: lumber and plywood factories; brewery in operation; the oyster beds along Puget Sound. Then have dinner at the Olympia Oyster House at the water's edge.

Speaking of state capitals, a good one to start with is your own. We take the places close to us for granted, but they often prove to have as much glamour as the distant horizon.

Traveling in Europe, one could be expected to go out of his way to visit great universities like Oxford and Heidelberg. Why not here in America as well? For youngsters on the educational upswing nothing could be better; nor are parents too old to acquire an appreciation of learning. Our national heritage is very much alive on the campus of a college or university, with its hallowed buildings, laboratories, museums, and landscaped grounds where you walk in the footsteps of American scholars.

Apart from the campus, college towns frequently are attractive in their own right. They can be pleasant, economical vacation spots, particularly since student haunts are inured to undergrad allowances.

All colleges welcome visitors and many furnish guide services. The Ivy League schools, to pick a group, are the oldest. Harvard, at Cambridge, the country's first university, was founded in 1636. The historic "Yard" represents the history of American architecture from colonial Massachusetts Hall (1720) through the nineteenth-century works of Bulfinch down to the contemporary style of Lamont Library (1949). The Harvard Library houses over six million volumes, including a Gutenberg Bible and treasured Shakespeare Folios.

Dartmouth, at Hanover, New Hampshire, has many handsome colonial buildings, notably on Dartmouth Row. Another point of interest is Baker Memorial Library, where immense murals by José Orozco (spread over 3000 feet of wall space) depict the story of civilization on the American continent. Yale, at New Haven, Connecticut, is distinguished by Connecticut Hall, its oldest building (1752), sole survivor of the legendary "Old Brick Row"; Memorial Quadrangle, a showplace of Gothic architecture in America; and Payne Whitney Gymnasium, the largest building in the world devoted to sports and physical training. At Brown University, Providence, Rhode Island, the oldest building was used during the Revolutionary War as a barracks and hospital, while the library contains one of the finest collections of Americana printed before 1800. The First Baptist Church, where commencements have been held since 1775, was organized by Roger Williams in 1638, and is the Baptist mother church in America. At Cornell's beautiful campus at Ithaca, New York, visitors are welcome to climb to the Clock Tower for the lofty view of Cayuga Lake.

The world's tallest school building, the Cathedral of Learning at the University of Pittsburgh, is 42 stories high; student guides conduct visitors on a miniature world tour through the 18 nationality rooms, each furnished in the style of a different country.

Thomas Jefferson's University of Virginia, founded as "an academical village," thrives now as a monument to his foresight. From the pantheon-like Rotunda, you can see the entire university as he designed it, the two colonnades of student quarters facing each other across a terraced lawn, bordered by slender serpentine walls and gardens.

Not all schools worth visiting are large ones. Washington and Lee University, at Lexington, Virginia, is a small college gem, its chapel a shrine and museum dedicated to Robert E. Lee, the university president following the Civil War. Virginia Military Institute, also in Lexington, is rich in the tradition of its heroes, from Stonewall Jackson to George C. Marshall.

Berea College, at Berea, Kentucky, is a most unusual school, designed to provide higher learning to youngsters of the Southern Highlands who cannot afford to go elsewhere. Its lovely campus is a veritable beehive, for all the students work—in offices, or the large college-owned farms, and at handcrafts. The Boone Tavern, well run and moderately priced ($6–$11 double), is staffed mainly by students. Paul Green's symphonic drama, *Wilderness Road*, is a summer feature at Berea.

Another pleasant university-operated hotel is the Carolina Inn, at Chapel Hill, North Carolina ($8–$10 double). Morehead Planetarium,

also a part of the University of North Carolina, is the only planetarium in the South. At Durham, Duke University, endowed by the Duke cigarette millions, is clearly one of the most beautiful places in America, renowned for its Gothic architecture and expansive gardens.

The Big Ten colleges of the Midwest are worth visiting too—and not just on football Saturdays. The University of Michigan, one of the oldest state colleges, has many fine buildings on its booming campus at Ann Arbor; its arboretum contains 2000 species of herbs, plants, and trees. The University of Wisconsin, at Madison, also has an outstanding arboretum of 1200 experimental acres, as large as the campus itself, on the shores of Lake Mendota. The Forest Products Laboratory, operated jointly with the U. S. Department of Agriculture, offers free guided tours.

In the Southwest, the University of Oklahoma, at Norman, displays extensive collections of Indian art and fossils of giant reptiles that once roamed the continent. At the University of Texas, at Austin, most buildings are in Spanish Renaissance style; while the University of New Mexico, at Albuquerque, is a study in pueblo style. But for rare architecture, visit Texas Western, at El Paso—it resembles a Tibetan monastery.

Leland Stanford University, at Palo Alto, California, has one of the largest and most interesting campuses in the Far West. Its principal sights include the Memorial Church, with a façade of mosaics brought from Italy; the art gallery, and the Herbert Hoover Library on War, Revolution, and Peace. From the library tower, 285 feet high, the visitor can see the area's growing industrial parks and the mountains of the Coast Range.

The service academies, schools of higher learning too, reflect the traditions and achievements of the military forces. West Point, on a rocky bluff overlooking the Hudson River, was used as a fort by the Americans during the Revolutionary War and has been the site of the Military Academy since 1802. The Coast Guard Academy is located, appropriately enough, at New London, Connecticut, port city and old whaling center. The Naval Academy, at Annapolis, Maryland, is an inspiring place, particularly on Wednesday afternoons when the middies march in dress parade. The newest of the academies, the Air Force's, was opened in the fall of 1958, on a beautiful 17,900-acre site at the foot of the Rocky Mountains north of Colorado Springs,

A section of the Leland Stanford University campus, Palo Alto, California, distinguished by its Spanish-influenced architecture and (in the background) 285-foot tower above the Hoover Library.

The Corps of Cadets parade in precision formation across the plain at West Point, New York, a military post since the Revolution. A hotel on the grounds is open to the public.

Colorado. You are welcome to drive through the grounds to see the handsome contemporary style buildings (Cadet Dormitory, Academic-Library Building, Aerodynamics Laboratory, Gymnasium, Spitz Planetarium) and to stop for lunch at the Community Center.

The service schools are by no means the only military bases open to the public. There is a great deal to be seen, learned, and enjoyed at many installations, which recount history, heroism, and methods of warfare from the crude musket to the push button.

The Air Force Museum, the largest display on aviation history in the world, is fittingly located at Dayton, Ohio, on the very ground over which the Wright Brothers made many of their earliest test flights. The museum, located at Wright-Patterson Air Force Base, houses 20,000 or more items, ranging from primitive planes and engines down through World War II aircraft and such recent creations as the Matador and Snark guided missiles, B-52 intercontinental jet bomber, F-107 fighter, and X-3, X-5, and X-10, all experimental supersonic craft. Photographs are permitted of any of the museum's exhibits.

Fort Knox, Kentucky, the training center of the Armored Corps, is the setting for the Army's George S. Patton Memorial Museum, dedicated to the famed World War II tank commander. It contains a col-

From the Wright Brothers to the Space Age, the Air Force Museum, at Dayton, Ohio, houses the world's largest aviation collection. The three historic aircraft on the lawn: P-47 Thunderbolt, X-3, and P-59.

lection of Axis military equipment and weapons, as well as General Patton's official jeep and trailer, his flags and trophies.

Fort Sill, Oklahoma, in contrast, recalls the thrilling period when it was commanded by General Phil Sheridan as an isolated cavalry post in the Indian country. The old guardhouse, built in 1871, was used to imprison the Kiowa war chiefs and later Geronimo himself. Fort Bliss, at El Paso, also figured in the Army's colorful western saga. One of its chief attractions is the replica of the old fort established in 1848 when a slender line of soldiers and settlers completed a historic 673-mile trek across the desert from San Antonio. Fort Bliss in time became famous as a cavalry post commanded by General Pershing during the Mexican War, and is now headquarters of the Army's guided missile program, affording visitors a close look at missiles, electronic and aircraft displays. Texas, and particularly San Antonio, is fabled military country. Fort Sam Houston contains many displays dating from its beginning as a replacement for the Alamo and its command by generals like Robert E. Lee, Pershing, and Wainwright. Randolph Field, "the showplace of the Air Force," includes the School of Aviation Medicine and the Crew Training Air Force, with everything in sight from helicopters to jet tankers.

While many of the western posts are associated with the Indian frontier days, the Presidio, at San Francisco, one of the most storied of them all, had its beginnings as a Spanish outpost. The original Presidio was built in 1776, later was taken by Mexico, and finally, in 1846, by the United States. The view from the Presidio, sitting like a crown atop the peninsula, is spectacular in all directions. Its officers' club, built of adobe brick, is the oldest building in San Francisco. Throughout the fort are markers indicating points of historic interest.

The Navy, too, has interesting stations open to the public. Two in Florida which offer guided tours are at Key West, a naval station since 1822 when it served as a base to combat Caribbean pirates (admission, 50¢; children under eight, free; tours at other stations are free), and Pensacola, the training ground of naval aviators. The largest operating base is at Norfolk, Virginia, where the Shipyard Museum houses a fortune in historic ships and models. And at Portsmouth, New Hampshire, where the war between Russia and Japan was ended in the Treaty of 1905, the Navy now concentrates its submarine training and operations.

Two of the newest landmarks are the Harry S. Truman Library and the Eisenhower Home and Museum. Regardless of your politics, both of these reflect the history of our time, in a sense transcending the individuals involved.

The beautiful crescent-shaped Truman Library at Independence, Missouri (9–4:30, 2–5 Sunday; 50¢; children under 12 free), is administered by the U. S. National Archives, although built and furnished from private donations amounting to $1,750,000. Besides its vast collection of papers and books, of value principally to scholars, it highlights the history of the Presidency with pictures and documents. The replica of the President's Office gives you the feeling of being in the White House—the furnishings are exact reproductions, the pictures, statuary and desk objects are the originals used in President Truman's administration. You will also see Mr. Truman's extensive collection of bibles, autographed photos and books from Winston Churchill and other world figures. Mr. Truman, who still lives in Independence, has his office in this building.

The Eisenhower Home and adjacent Museum at Abilene, Kansas (9–5, home, free; Museum, 50¢, children, 25¢) recount the complete story of Dwight Eisenhower's rise from boyhood through his military career. Because the family home, the rambling two-story frame house on 4th Street, became available so early, all the items are original. Even Mother Eisenhower's potted palms thrive in the front parlor where she cared for them until her death in 1946. The modern $400,000

Museum contains over 3,000 items associated with Dwight D. Eisenhower, his mementoes, medals of war, gifts from all over the world. The oldest: an 8th Century B. C. wine urn from Greece. Notice the site directly across the street—the Eisenhower Library will be erected there.

Besides these types of travel objectives, you can tour Civil War battlefields, caves, antique automobile museums. You can't take them away, as you can antiques and sea shells, but they lend a purpose and a theme to your travels.

Even cemeteries have a certain travel appeal. They account for noted works of sculpture and landscaping. Arlington National Cemetery is the best known and most visited, followed by Gettysburg. Rock Creek Cemetery, the oldest in the national capital, contains the sculptured figure, commonly called Grief, by Saint-Gaudens, which Alexander Woolcott described as the most perfect thing fashioned by the hand of man, and the Ffoulke Memorial, Rabboni, by Gutzon Borglum. The burial place of Francis Scott Key at Mount Olivet Cemetery, Frederick, Maryland, is one of the few places where the American flag is never lowered. Ignominy in death: the graves of the six "raiders" placed apart from their prison comrades at Andersonville, Georgia. Southern California visitors find Forest Lawn, in Glendale, so interesting that many spend hours viewing its gardens, marble statues, precious gem collection, stained-glass reproduction of The Last Supper, and the Wee Kirk of the Heather.

In Cedar Rapids, the Turner Mortuary has the largest display of original paintings by the celebrated Iowa artist, Grant Wood.

Art, Americana, and beauty are where you find them.

8

Industry's Open House

A ringside seat at a great American spectacle, absolutely free, is the treat visitors receive when they join a plant tour to see industry at work. The range covers everything from sugar to steel, chocolate bars to motor cars, and beside the absorbing educational experience, there frequently are refreshments, souvenirs, or booklets as mementos of the visit.

The plant tour is one facet of industry's new look. Instead of the

old grimy, smoke-stained structures, the modern factory is attractive and landscaped. To the sponsoring company, the plant tour is one means of advertising and building good will; to the economy-conscious family looking for worth-while places to visit, it is made to order.

There are several ways of learning the location of available plant tours. Some are well publicized. Chambers of commerce generally have a directory of plant tours in their areas. Or when you write the official information agency of a state you are planning to visit, ask about them. Try to obtain tour schedules so you won't arrive at the wrong time or the wrong day. If you have children, avoid disappointment by determining in advance whether they are old enough for the particular tour you have in mind. If you have the chance and know your dates, write the factory.

Of the hundreds of factory tours offered along the principal travel routes, here are a few suggestions for your vacation itinerary:

Automobiles: All the major companies offer conducted tours, so you can follow the car of your choice as it takes shape along the assembly line. The tours usually last forty-five to ninety minutes. At Dearborn, Ford features the most extensive tour program in its Rotunda, the largest industrial exhibition building in the world, and at the mammoth River Rouge plant. The Rotunda includes displays on research and engineering; visitors are driven over the adjacent one-mile test track in new cars. All conducted tours of the Rouge plant originate at the Rotunda aboard company buses; Monday through Friday, 9–3:30. The country's largest free antique automobile museum, the Thompson Products Auto Album at Cleveland, Ohio, presents an intriguing array of cars dating to the 1890s. It also presents aviation displays. Open every day, 11–5; Sunday, 1–5.

Chocolate: Hershey Chocolate Corporation, Hershey, Pennsylvania, provides 40-minute guided tours, Monday through Friday, except first two weeks in July. Also in Hershey: zoo, gardens (both free), and a museum of colonial and Pennsylvania Dutch items, 75¢, children under 12 free.

Coal: The Pocahontas Exhibition Mine, Pocahontas, Virginia, near Bluefield, West Virginia, shows rich coal seams up to 10 feet thick in a cavernous tunnel. Mine equipment—coal cutters, rails, cars—is shown at intervals, and signs explain the various steps in mining. The Exhi-

The Ford Rotunda, Dearborn, Michigan, where visitors are driven over the adjacent test track and then guided on tours of the mammoth River Rouge automobile plant.

bition Mine is perpetually cool, a relief from summer heat. Open 8–5; guides on advance notice. Admission, 25¢; children, 15¢.

Electric Appliances: General Electric at its fabulous Appliance Park, Louisville, Kentucky, offers guided tours to delight the housewife, for here you see gleaming new refrigerators, ranges, dishwashers, disposals, and other contrivances that make modern living more pleasant produced at the rate of one every 2½ seconds. At the model kitchen you see the latest in styling, color, accessory furnishings. Appliance Park's 950 acres include 200 acres in grass, an arboretum of 11,000 trees and shrubs. Regular tours start at the Main Gate Monday through Friday at 1:30 P.M.

Glass: The Corning Glass Center, Corning, New York, presents the story of man's creative achievement with a single material—glass, from the earliest vessels fashioned by the Egyptians to the most modern adaptations. In the lobby of the Center is the largest piece of glass ever made: the original 200-inch telescope mirror disk, twin to the one at Palomar Observatory in California. The Corning Museum houses one of the most extensive collections of glass in the world; the Hall of Science exhibits glass in its versatility—lighter than cork, as heavy as iron. Galleries enable visitors to witness glass blowers carrying on an ancient craft in producing the cherished, graceful Steuben glass. Open every day except Monday, 9:30–5.

Iron: At the Mesabi Range, Minnesota, where most of the world's iron is mined, eight observation stands are conveniently located for visitors. The famous Hull-Rust-Mahoning Mine, at Hibbing, is over 400 feet deep and has its own 55-mile railroad. The Oliver Mining Division of U. S. Steel operates its own rail system in the Mesabi Range with 95 locomotives and over 575 cars, signals and shops. In the summer samples of pure iron ore can be had for the asking.

Marble and Granite: Visit the world's largest granite quarry, Rock of Ages, at Graniteville, Vermont, 8 miles long, 4 miles wide, and 10 miles deep. Here granite is cut from its bed by powerful channeling machines, then sent to the mills to be sawed into slabs by smooth steel band saws. At the finishing shops, artisans cut and carve the granite into mantels, statues, memorials. Open May 1 to the end of November; the finishing plant open Monday through Friday, 8:30–4. The Marble Exhibit of the Vermont Marble Company at Proctor, the largest in the country, includes no less than 60 displays of full-scale interior installations, tiled bathrooms, fireplaces, garden furniture, and a bas-relief of Da Vinci's Last Supper carved from a single block of marble. Open from June 1 to mid-October, 9–5. Georgia marble: most of it is produced at Elberton in northeastern Georgia, where visitors are welcome at quarries and shops. Missouri marble: Carthage, in the Ozarks, produces marble known for hardness and durability. Indiana limestone: at Bedford, visit the Indiana Limestone Institute and one of the quarries which have produced stone for some of the nation's tallest and finest buildings.

Photography: The Eastman Kodak plant at Rochester, New York, shows many sides of camera and lens. The 50-room George Eastman Museum, now an independent institution chartered by New York State, depicts the first experiments of men like Daguerre and Fox Talbot. On one floor visitors can turn the handle of an 1895 Mutoscope peepshow and view animated stills, precursor of the motion picture, and on another floor see modern color film of sun eruptions. Guided tours are conducted at the Camera Works and Hawk-Eye Works Monday through Friday at 10 A.M. and 2 P.M. and at the Kodak Park Works at 9:30 A.M. and 1:30 P.M.

Pickles, and 56 other varieties: It's more fun than you think to watch a lowly cucumber rise to a high-level pickle. Touring the H. J. Heinz plant in Pittsburgh takes about an hour, plus time for a movie and a snack sampling. Monday through Friday, 8:30–10:30 and 1–2:30.

Rubber: At Akron, Goodyear shows visitors its little pioneer factory, where in 1898 carriage tires and horseshoe pads were made, and the huge modern plant manufacturing nearly 100 types of tires, fabric boats, and other rubber products. The Rubber Exhibit in Goodyear Hall dramatizes the history of rubber from the discovery of vulcanizing to its diverse uses today. Trips through the Plant 1 "tire cycle" start from the Rubber Exhibit at 9 A.M. and 2 P.M. Monday through Friday. The Goodyear Blimp Base is located on nearby Wingfoot Lake. Firestone conducts tours to its tire plant No. 1, Research Laboratory, and famous Historical Exposition. The tours begin every day, Monday through Friday, at 2 P.M. from the fifth floor lobby of the Clock Tower Building, 1200 Firestone Parkway.

· Very Important: Minimum age, 12, at both rubber factories. Note also minimum age at steel plants. Other plant tours listed do not have an age restriction.

Steel: United States Steel conducts tours at four plants, as follows: Pittsburgh, every Wednesday morning by bus from its downtown office building to the Homestead Works. The 1½-hour tour includes open hearth operation, slab mill, and plate mill. For reservations, write Public Relations, U. S. Steel, 525 William Penn Place, Pittsburgh 30, Pennsylvania (minimum age, 16). Birmingham, Tuesday and Wednesday morning, October through May. Guests report at the Fairfield

Works main entrance, board buses to visit blast furnace, open hearth, blooming mill, and strip mill. Each visitor receives small box of assorted nails as a souvenir. Write Public Relations, U. S. Steel, 1429 Brown-Marx Building, Birmingham, Alabama (minimum age, 12). Provo, Utah, Monday through Friday, tours of one of the West's largest steel plants, at the foot of Lake Timpanogos. Write Public Relations, Geneva Division, U. S. Steel, Provo, Utah. Iron Mountain, Minnesota, the experimental Pilotac taconite plant, processing hard rock containing low-grade iron ore. Kaiser Steel conducts tours at its plant at Fontana, California, 47 miles from Los Angeles, 38 miles from Disneyland. Tours last 2½ hours, Monday through Friday and three evenings. Write Public Relations, Kaiser Steel, Fontana, California (minimum age, 11).

Submarines: The Submarine Library, on the banks of the Thames River, Groton, Connecticut, is maintained by the Electric Boat Division of General Dynamics Corporation. Exhibits trace the development of submarines from the hand-powered wooden Groton-built "Turtle" of the American Revolution down to Electric Boat's modern nuclear-powered roamer of the deep. You can look through a periscope from here and see submarines on the river and the Navy's principal sub base at New London on the opposite shore. Open 9–5 daily except Sunday.

Sugar: The country's largest raw cane plant is the Sugar House of the U. S. Sugar Corporation, Clewiston, Florida, on Route 80, between the Everglades and Lake Okeechobee. From 30,000 surrounding cane field acres, stalks are ground to molasses and raw sugar for shipment to the refinery at Savannah. From sugar to purebreds: adjacent Sugarland Ranch, which the company also operates, is a cross-breeding ground of Brahmans with Herefords, Anguses, and Shorthorns. Clewiston, on the shores of Lake Okeechobee, is an attractive community, starting point for fishing in the big lake and swamp buggy rides in the Everglades.

Trees: Tree farms, new and widespread, cover 45 million acres in 46 states. Wood-using industries are spending more than $56 million yearly in their management and development. A visit to a tree farm discloses the forest as a living community—of trees, other plants, wildlife, and water, each dependent on the other and on the understanding care which man alone can give. A trip through a wood-using industry unlocks the mysteries of how wood becomes paper, lumber,

Industry at work: a group of visitors around the tour conductor at the blast furnace of the United States Steel Fairfield Works, Birmingham, Alabama. U. S. Steel offers guided tours at four of its major plants.

plywood, veneer, or eventually the furniture we use. Tree farms are usually well posted. For information on both farms and lumber plants, write the American Forest Products Industries, Inc., 1816 N Street, N.W., Washington 6, D.C. Booklets covering several states individually are available.

Many timberlands have been opened as public parks with camping and other facilities. In Oregon alone there are 16 parks, with such features as the world's biggest Douglas fir tree; a memorial to the only Americans killed by enemy action on United States soil in World War II (by a Japanese balloon bomb explosion); and a short course in tree identification.

9

The Sport of Touring, Revived

In the early days of motoring, so we are told, it was fun to get behind the wheel and drive someplace, no matter where. Of course, the "good old days" always improve with age, but touring evidently was an adventurous type of how-to-do-it sport. Members of the driving set repaired their own cars (through necessity as well as choice) and on a cross-country run would send a "pathfinder" ahead to mark the course by painting telephone poles or strewing confetti in the road. Part of the sport involved a little "catch me" game with local police, challenging 20 or 25 mile speed limits. This usually ended with an arrest and fine—and a sense of satisfaction!

Such thrills are lacking now. Hardly anyone, except for the antique-car collector and the sports-car fan, understands what makes his automobile tick or enjoys the sheer sport of driving on the open road. The fellow in the neighborhood who takes time to get under the hood of his car, or to wax it, is almost suspect.

In a sense, all this is too bad. There ought to be the same romance in the road and in one's car, for, despite highway congestion and inner mechanical complications, motoring in our day is safer and more comfortable, its horizons much broader than in the lamented past.

The truth is that driving, the time spent behind the wheel, can be a pleasant part of a vacation trip, if you give it half a chance. And you

Idaho Route 15, a new soil-cement road from Boise to the Payette Lakes sports area, indicates the capability of modern highway building. The muddy, rutted, dusty road—the bane of the motor tourist—has been eliminated, even in the back country.

can reduce your travel costs by knowing something about your car, or at least by taking a little interest in caring for it and driving it properly. Automobile operation in dollars and cents totals about 20 per cent, or slightly more, of your total vacation expense, so there is a substantial amount of money involved. In fact, you may be able to decrease your gasoline consumption by five more miles per gallon— $10 saved during a thousand mile trip, enough for a good dinner or an extra night's lodging.

FOR BETTER FUEL CONSUMPTION

Avoid these habits:

1. Fast starts and quick stops in traffic.

Cultivate these:

1. Ease off on the gasoline when you see a red light—it may change so you do not have to stop at all.

2. High speed driving on the open road.

2. Hold a safe, normal speed of 60 or 65 at the most.

3. Buying expensive, high-grade fuels, unless recommended in the manual issued by the manufacturer of your car. Motor fuels are so refined the regular grade is now superior to the best of a few years ago.

3. Rely on standard-grade gasoline. Most cars will do just as well. You may lose a little in pick-up, but you reach the destination just as soon.

4. Driving with underinflated tires.

4. Have tire pressure checked every time you buy gasoline.

Start by taking care of your car before you set out for distant parts. If you think it is difficult in your home town to find a competent garageman who doesn't charge an arm and a leg, just wait till you are on the road. With car trouble away from home the odds are all against you; you may pay as much as 50 to 100 per cent more, to say nothing of spending frustrating waiting time in a strange garage when you could be enjoying your vacation. So have your car checked thoroughly. A motor tune up alone will give you better consumption and smoother driving; new plugs, if they are needed, will pay for themselves in a few thousand miles. Have the garageman lubricate your car and check brakes, ignition system, windshield wipers, steering gear, lights, and battery. Wheel balance and front-end alignment are important too; a wheel out of alignment wastes gas, shortens tire life, and reduces driving safety. If your tires are wearing thin, shop around and replace them before you leave.

You do not need to change oil every 1000 or 1500 miles if your car is equipped with a good filter. An oil change is less necessary in long distance touring than in local stop-go driving. One manufacturer now concedes an oil change every 4000 miles will suffice, with a good filter, except under dusty conditions.

Your car should be in excellent condition for fast driving anywhere, but especially on turnpikes where high speeds can be maintained steadily for hours. If your car is aging and in questionable condition, steer clear of turnpikes. At steady speeds over 50 miles per hour radiators boil, engines throw rods, steering and brakes may fail, and worn tires blow out. Add to this the high cost of towing when you break down miles from a service station.

There is wisdom in car care. Minimum towing charge on the New York Thruway, $5; maximum, $10; midnight to 6 A.M., 50 per cent extra.

Check your gasoline gauge before you drive on a turnpike; you will probably pay more at a turnpike filling station. And should you run out of gasoline you will be delayed needlessly until you're spotted by a patrol car.

Note the accompanying table on the leading causes of breakdown in one year on the New York Thruway. Many could easily have been avoided; the others emphasize the importance of a thorough car checkup.

COSTLY MOTORING MISCUES

Ten Leading Causes of Arrest on New York Thruway		*Why Cars Break Down*	
From Annual Report of New York State Thruway Authority		*Principal Causes of Thruway Road Service*	
1. Speeding	22,638	Out of gasoline	16,178
2. License violation	1,814	Flat tire or blowout	14,905

3. Equipment violation   1,304
   (lights, horn, etc.)
4. Registration violation   1,064
5. Failure to comply with
   trooper's orders   433
6. Failure to keep right   418
7. U turn   418
8. Parking   287
9. One-way traffic violation   229
10. Changing lanes unsafely   223

Ignition trouble   3,062
Water required   2,600
Unable to start motor   1,625
Fan belt broken   1,284
Out of oil   1,071

Driving with worn tires may cost more than the price of replacements. In one year, almost 25 per cent of all fatal accidents on the Pennsylvania Turnpike were caused by tire trouble.

Should you travel the turnpike route? The toll roads are fast, direct routes with a minimum of confusion. They bypass congested city traffic, are free of annoying stop lights, intersections, and steep grades. Undoubtedly, over long distances they save time. There is no denying that turnpikes are safe roads, at least by comparison. Every toll road is thoroughly patrolled, its speed limit strictly enforced. On almost all the turnpikes drivers are notified by large neon signs or from mobile loudspeakers of reduced speed limits when required by fog, ice or other weather conditions. Should you include one or more turnpikes in your itinerary, do not fail to allow for the toll in your budget. Incidentally, for 25¢, you can now purchase emergency breakdown service insurance at toll gates on the New York Thruway and Pennsylvania Turnpike (possibly others soon) covering up to $25 charges and valid for a 48-hour period.

With the advancement of the Interstate Highway System, free expressways—having the same characteristics as the toll roads—are appearing all over the country. Familiarize yourself with them. Before you set out, look your maps over carefully to determine whether a free superhighway will serve you as well as a toll road. Interstate-type roads are as safe, and sometimes safer, since they incorporate latest engineering features.

The Interstate System in time will involve 41,000 miles of high speed, controlled-access highways connecting 90 per cent of all cities with 50,000 or more population. About twenty-five per cent, or 10,000 miles, is already open to your use. These pointers will help in following the new route numbers appearing on red, white and blue shields:

1. Odd numbers indicate North-South routes. U. S. 95, for instance, is the Interstate Route from Maine to Florida (supplanting the old Route 1). Even numbers indicate East-West routes. The trans-continental numbers: 10, 20, 40, 70, 80, 90.

2. You may see Interstate numbers on a 200-mile stretch, then not again for another thousand, so keep track of the old route numbers on the black and white shield, too.

Sustained high speed driving *is* different than your normal daily stint behind the wheel. Keep pace with traffic, neither much faster nor slower. To stay alert, eat lightly. Stop for a breather after the first three hours of travel—and every 100 miles thereafter. The respite will benefit the driver and everyone in the car. Plan a roadside lunch as one of these stops; this will be a timesaver, considering that during peak periods you may have to wait for service at turnpike restaurants.

How far should you plan to travel? Set a daily limit of 450 miles at the most. Driving at high speed is one thing, but driving at high speed when you're tired is quite another.

This point will encourage you to limit your driving hours: expect to cover a greater distance—possibly one-fourth more—in the same period of time than you covered three or five years ago. This is due largely to the elimination of city bottlenecks. For example, you can drive north to south through Denver, a distance of 11 miles, without dropping below 50 miles an hour. In Los Angeles five years ago it took 30 minutes from downtown to suburban Whittier; today you can reach Disneyland, twice as far, in that same 30 minutes.

These expressway and by-pass improvements have been completed not only in the West, but everywhere: Atlanta, Baltimore, Boston, Philadelphia, Pittsburgh, Chicago, Kansas City, and others are underway in almost every metropolitan area.

To increase your mileage, gas consumption and safety, travel when highway traffic is lightest. Statistics show that Saturday is the week's worst day for accidents and Sunday the second worst.

Pick a weekday, any weekday, and start early—say at 7 A.M., before the local rush hour begins. The prettiest, most inspiring hour of day is morning twilight; it is also the coolest hour during the summer. Stop early, too, especially before evening twilight; the shadows become deceptive and tricky after a day behind the wheel.

For the real sport of touring think of the pursuit of the open road as part of the vacation experience; moderate your speed, observe and enjoy the countryside, its landscape, the villages and their architecture. These are the hidden glories of America that ask to be seen and appreciated.

Now we can travel the lesser roads in confidence, for there are none of the dirt-surfaced, muddy, rutted, unmarked paths the early motorists were forced to use. Even in the back country, or what's left of it, roads are in good repair. And here is the last refuge of the genuine tourist, who proceeds his unhurried, unharried way, admiring and enjoying the scenery, stopping to read the historical markers, looking for distinctive eating places, passing the time of day with the locals, learning from them of an attractive inn or an uncrowded camping area.

This is the way to utilize your car as a vacation vehicle; to scout the country for yourself and discover friendly communities; to explore the lesser known national monuments and state parks, locating outstanding areas which are no longer remote and inaccessible but which still give you the sense of finding something new.

An excellent example of this type road is U. S. 93, newly hard-surfaced for 61 miles from Sun Valley north to the Stanley Basin, one of the West's most colorful, scenic regions. An overlook at Galena Summit (8750 feet) faces the towering peaks of the Sawtooth Mountains; access roads (unpaved but passable) lead to campgrounds and lodges at the shores of sparkling Redfish and Stanley Lakes.

Such modern mountain roads are easy to drive, gently graded, engineered for safety. Even the older mountain roads can be part of your driving adventure. Just take it a little slower than usual. Relax, stop at overlooks and enjoy the scenery. Stay on the right, particularly heading into a curve; if it's a blind curve, honk your horn to warn any motorist who may be coming from the opposite direction. Use lower gears on steep downgrades—engine compression helps to save your brakes. Keep your radiator filled; water boils at lower temperature at higher elevations.

The station wagon, while not exactly new, is enjoying a surge of popularity as a vacation vehicle. Not since the wide-fendered old touring cars have the manufacturers provided so much space for long-distance driving. The station wagon is so flexible that a couple on the go can live in it completely without need of even a tent or a fireplace. Even for a family of four, the station wagon provides room for all their gear with plenty of space left over.

Utilize your station wagon to the fullest. With children you can adapt the interior as a play area by putting the middle seats down, or as a bedroom, spreading two inflated air mattresses over the open middle area. For outdoor cooking, set up your stove, cooler, and food container on the tail gate and cook waist-high as in your own kitchen. Take advantage of the space on top, too. Buy (or build) a car-top luggage carrier for your tent and other gear, but be sure to cover it with waterproof canvas.

With a station wagon properly managed you have the edge in seeking uncongested motoring. No matter what type your vehicle, however, look for those less crowded driving hours and routes, for they prove pleasant and more economical.

While you are on the highway, pay heed to the signs citing anti-litter laws. Many states and communities mean business with their warnings of stiff fines and penalties. To toss litter is at best a poor personal practice, at its worst the cause of an expensive ($50 million) national cleanup bill. Avoid the possibility of an arrest and fine by including a trash bag as standard equipment in your car and by disposing of your litter properly at service stations or roadside trash receptacles.

10

Friends Who Help You Save

The All-Year Club of Southern California is an institution which makes a practice of giving. It mails tons of literature and millions of words of guidance, while at its Los Angeles office the staff welcomes a visitor by presenting him with a large, full-color sight-seeing map; six "Motorlogs" outlining self-guided trips around Los Angeles; a monthly calendar of events; free TV tickets; a 44-page guide to Southern California hotels, motels, and resorts; and a variety of helpful folders assembled in communities from Topaz Lake to Calexico. Besides all this, an attractive, able young lady known as a "Welcomette" gives all the time needed to map out a personalized itinerary and answer questions on touring in Southern California.

What makes the All-Year Club so generous? It is the promotion organization for a giant-size vacation industry, which realizes that luring visitors to California is only one part of its job; insuring an enjoyable stay is the other half, since there is still no more effective advertising than a satisfied customer. The visitor is the principal beneficiary, for having taken the time to seek expert advice, he proceeds to save money, to utilize his vacation time to best advantage, and to understand the places he sees, rather than flying blind.

Among similar organizations are the Colorado Visitors Bureau and city promotional agencies in New York, Boston, Philadelphia, Washington, D.C., Miami and Miami Beach, Cleveland, Chattanooga, Knoxville, San Diego and San Francisco. Address them as Convention and Visitors Bureau (Californians, Inc., for San Francisco).

There are many sources worth contacting, both before you travel and along the way. All of them are in business to help you. In one way or another you probably pay for the service they provide—buying products, paying local taxes, and patronizing their sponsors—so don't hesitate to call on them.

If you are a member of the American Automobile Association contact your local office before you leave. Membership is a sound travel investment. Ask for tour books and accommodations directories as well as the triptiks (marked strip maps). Call on affiliated clubs for service en route.

Otherwise, contact one of the major oil companies. They spend millions of dollars in developing road maps and touring services for your guidance. They distribute 160,000,000 maps a year, so you need not hesitate to ask for yours. Following are four of the best services and how to use them:

Texaco—stop at an affiliated service station and fill out a "routing request card," which the dealer forwards to the Texaco Touring Service. You will receive in the mail a set of marked maps, 32-page booklet of helpful travel tips, and motel directories. Touring centers, where you may stop in for information, are located in New York, New Orleans, Chicago, Houston, Los Angeles.

Esso—operates on a similar basis. Visit a local dealer for a trip request card, which he will mail for you to the Esso Touring Service. Or visit touring centers in New York, Washington, New Orleans.

Shell—offers same type service available through dealers only. Shell is preparing an extensive plan (possibly in effect when you read this) whereby local dealers can supply detailed information on points of interest and accommodations everywhere.

Gulf—provides maps, motel guide and log book in its package. Gulf "Tourgide" maps are helpful in touring major cities, citing routes and principal points of interest. Ask for them at dealers or Tourgide bureaus in Boston, New York, Philadelphia, Pittsburgh, Toledo, Atlanta, New Orleans, Houston.

Follow the travel advertisements in newspapers and magazines. Most of the literature offered in the ads is intended to give practical information, as well as attract vacation trade. Free travel literature is costly to prepare and the people who pay for it have learned their investment is best returned when they give something useful, readable, and attractive to their potential visitors.

Travel with a credit card—or should you? In a certain sense, the credit card is the most useful invention since the traveler's check many years ago. It is easy to obtain one, if your credit is good at home, and you will find these advantages:

· You carry less cash, lower the risk of loss on your trip.
· You get a monthly statement, providing a record of trip costs.
· The guidebook you receive lists a variety of overnight accommodations, restaurants and other services for you to choose from.
· You will have identification and evidence of financial responsibility should you need it in emergency.

On the other hand, there are disadvantages, too, which every vacation traveler should understand. The credit card, you recall, was

A friendly port of call, the Savannah Chamber of Commerce, in the historic Cotton Exchange Building.

devised for the businessman. It serves him very well in keeping tab on his expense account and tax declaration. But credit induces you to spend more money—after all, it's so simple to sign your name—than if you were spending hard cash out of your pocket. Many hotels, motels and restaurants, at first delighted with the promotion and business they expected from credit card affiliation, have become disenchanted with the five to ten per cent commission they must pay. A new practice for them is to add this amount to the bill and offer you a discount for cash—which they prefer. You will need a certain amount of cash in any event. There is still nothing wrong with travelers' checks; you pay a slight charge but it's worth it to eliminate carrying cash. And no responsible establishment will look glassy-eyed at the customer offering a travelers' check.

By all means, travel with one or more oil company credit cards. If you decide on getting the other cards, and don't mind the fee, carry two or three if you intend to travel extensively on credit. These are the principal cards, their individual features, and how to obtain them:

CREDIT CARD	COST	FEATURES	HOW TO SECURE ONE
Oil Company	Free	Buy gas and oil, automotive repairs at affiliated stations.	Apply your nearest favorite station.
American Express	$6; $3 for additional members of family or firm.	Charge account valid at hotels, motels, restaurants, night clubs; also car-rental agencies, automotive repair stations (Ford, G.M., Chrysler), florists, specialty stores. Includes world-wide hotel, motel reservation service. Charge transportation tickets through any American Express office or accredited travel agents. Central billing.	Any of 40 American Express offices, or from main office, 65 Broadway, New York City.
Carte Blanche (subsidiary of Hilton Hotels)	$6; no cost for use only at Hilton Hotels.	Valid at 33 Hilton Hotels and motor inns this country and abroad, selected others. Charge for meals, gifts, tickets, car rentals; check cashing.	Any Hilton Hotel.
Diners' Club	$5; $2.50 for additional members of family or firm.	Recommended restaurants, hotels, motels, night clubs, car rental, gift shops; 2000 automotive repair stations. Provides handy wallet-size guide booklet listing participating establishments. Central billing. Worldwide. Charge transportation through accredited travel agents.	Diners' Club, 10 Columbus Circle, New York 19, N.Y., or 30 branch offices.

When in doubt about the way, ask the operator of a service station (well kept, that is). He knows the road and will provide a map to show it.

Once underway you will find friendly ports of call. Chambers of commerce are among the best, for many of them furnish maps and literature, even arrange overnight reservations. Some chambers, like the one at Joplin, Missouri, in the Ozarks, offer guided tours. Others are tourist attractions themselves: the chamber of commerce at Savannah, Georgia, occupies the historic Cotton Exchange on Factors Walk. Convention and Visitors Bureaus, such as those in New York (facing Grand Central Station) and Washington, are also operated to furnish direction and information. So are the hospitality centers maintained by states and cities. Florida alone spends $300,000 to run its seven welcome stations at the principal points of entry to the state, where visitors are greeted with travel booklets, latest bulletins on road conditions, and a tall glass of orange juice.

Texas operates seven excellent Highway Information Bureaus at its borders to furnish maps, literature and touring guidance. And if you're traveling the Pennsylvania Turnpike you will find one blue-

and-gold Tourist Information trailer at the Ohio border and another at the New Jersey border, stocked with information on suggested tours off the Turnpike.

Or you can ask a police officer. Motorists diligently avoid policemen, although most officers would much rather give a helping hand than a ticket for a traffic violation. "Hospitality in Person . . . the Kentucky Trooper," is the descriptive term in the Kentucky state guide and map. "Your friend, the Kentucky Trooper, is on duty to protect you and serve you," the booklet advises. "He is as anxious to provide information or assistance when you need help as he is determined to enforce the traffic laws and regulations designed to keep Kentucky highways safe for you to travel. Don't hesitate to call on the Kentucky Trooper for assistance or information. To safeguard the lives of everybody, Kentucky driving rules and regulations should be carefully observed." This same attitude of fairness and readiness to help holds true in every state. Stop a state police car sometime and talk with the fellows. First, you will find they're glad to have the opportunity for conversation—a welcome interlude in cruising the highways. Next they will prove courteous and intelligent, willing and able to furnish guidance.

Some cities with a large tourist trade give their visitors free parking and a warning rather than an arrest or fine for a traffic violation, but almost anywhere—except in speed-trap territory—the average police officer prefers to fill a friendly role.

11

Contrast:
Nuisances of the Road

Your vacation money probably did not come easily to you. Even if it did, you are entitled to receive, full value for every dollar you spend. It hurts to be "taken." Yet the vacationing family unfortunately is a target. Be alert and cautious with your money.

One of the worst highway rackets is the speed trap, most prevalent in southern Georgia. It is usually operated in a small town with low revenue and low taxes, where the sheriff or chief of police is directed to collect the budget for the police department, possibly for the entire town government, through fines levied against out-of-state motorists. Sometimes the chief's salary, like the tax collector's, is based on commission—the more arrests the more money he earns. The same is true of the justice of the peace; his income is based on commission too.

Under these circumstances, what are the chances of winning a case on its merits? None at all, and the more commotion you create the more money you are likely to pay. In fine or forfeited collateral it costs anywhere from $10 to $75, although far worse are the sheer indignity and the discovery of such a mockery of law enforcement.

Suggested rules if you're caught in a speed trap: don't argue with the officer or the justice of the peace—their minds are made up; pay your fine and go on your way. The chances of recouping your loss are very slim, but you should vent your protest—through the right channel. Do not write, wire or phone a state official; his political future depends far more on tolerating the speed trap than on winning your friendship for his state. He may respond with tender words, but they're essentially from a form letter. The best bet is to call or write the chamber of commerce or daily newspaper in the nearest large city. These groups are embarrassed by outbursts of provincial inhospitality, which damages the reputation, and consequently the business, of the entire area. One editor was so chagrined with an outrageous speed trap arrest that he mailed the victim the amout of the fine out of his own pocket.

You can avoid inferior attractions and tourist "traps" by visiting only points of interest of reputation and stature. Steer clear of free highway zoos, which often prove to contain a gambling table next to the snake pit—and at this one you never win and have little recourse. In fact, why visit any highway zoo? If you want to see animals, there are zoological gardens of distinction in Boston, New York, Philadelphia, Washington, Chicago, St. Louis, New Orleans, San Francisco, San Diego, San Antonio and other cities. Several have areas designed specially for children. Try *them* sometime.

Ever notice those "free information" booths as you near a large city? Most of them are not affiliated with the chamber of commerce or visitors bureau. Rely on the official agencies for guidance. If you need information on the road, check with the nearest service station or police patrol.

Be careful in the vicinity of Mammoth Cave National Park, Kentucky. Vacationers headed to the national park are met on the road at what appears to be a ranger station by "official" guides in uniform, who sell tickets and lead them to a commercially operated, and inferior, cave. If you are visiting Mammoth Cave, be wary; tour tickets are sold only at park headquarters, not along the road.

Gambling ruses and games of chance sometimes come to light at roadside eating places. It seems harmless at first to try a punchboard or pegboard for the price of the meal, but when you suddenly discover the stakes are up to $200 you're in for trouble. Stay on the alert; don't risk even the smallest gambling investment at an unlikely place on the road.

An unpleasant irritant is the shocking condition motorists find at many service-station rest rooms. Surveys have shown that nearly 40 per cent are unclean or filthy and unfit for public use. They constitute a near menace to health, as well as an eyesore, with their stopped-up plumbing, broken water faucets, dirty washbowls, soapless soap dispensers, and lack of paper towels. In many cases they need both fumigation and a good scrubbing.

Generally speaking, stations operated and franchised by major oil companies try to maintain a high level of cleanliness. These firms realize that rest rooms have come to be as much a part of the equipment of service as the gasoline pump and the cash register. They are facilities the management should keep spotless; thoughtless motorists do contribute to filthy conditions, but where rest rooms are cleaned frequently their equipment is usually respected by the users.

Some oil companies stress sanitation through periodic inspections and sometimes by warning they will disfranchise a dealer who allows his rest rooms to get filthy. Should you experience a particularly bad situation, don't hesitate to cite it the next time you pay your credit card account.

12

The Vacation Ledger

Have you ever figured a vacation budget before leaving home? It's a lot easier than you think, especially if you are already in the habit of budgeting your normal living expenses. A budget provides useful guidelines, and by keeping track of actual expenses once you are underway, you will develop handy data for planning future trips.

These are the factors to consider:

| Car costs | Lodgings | Tolls | Souvenirs |
| Food | Admissions, entry fees | Tips | Incidentals |

VACATION LEDGER

How to Figure, Where to Save

Date	Mileage Reading	Car Costs 21%				Food and Meals 28%			Lodgings 23%	Entry Fees and Recreation 7%	Souvenirs and Purchases 15%	Tips	Tolls	Roadside Refreshments	Miscellaneous
		Gasoline		Oil		Repairs	Break-fast	Lunch	Dinner						6%	
		Gals.	Cost	Qts.	Cost											
Per cent of Average Vacation Expense																
		Estimate 4¢ per mile, $40 for 1000 mile trip; cultivate good driving habits to save on fuel; check car before departure to avoid possible excessive repair bills en route.					Your largest expenditure: $20 a day for family of four with all restaurant meals. Try light lunches at roadside parks. The more meals you prepare, the lower your expense.			$12 a day (family) at hotel or motel, almost nil with camping, but don't forget to list fees.	Resort hotels provide "built-in" recreation; touring, select attractions wisely.	Buy from reputable shops, as at home.	Be fair, but judicious.	Check car, gasoline before driving toll road.	Carry thermos, with your own beverages, especially with children.	Incidentals can really add up!—photo supplies, post cards, suntan oil, etc.

Start with your car expenses. Figure that with new gas taxes the average is now 4¢ a mile for gas and oil, or $40 for a 1000-mile trip. This covers only the operating costs and assumes that with a pre-trip checkup you won't require maintenance en route. To calculate more closely how many miles *your* car travels on a gallon of gasoline, follow this one-month test:

On your next visit to your service station fill your gasoline tank and record the speedometer reading and the number of gallons purchased; when you fill your tank again record only the number of gallons; at the end of the month record the speedometer reading again. Divide the difference between the two speedometer readings by the total number of gallons you have recorded.

For a family of four, food will probably be the largest single expense. If you go camping or stay in a cabin, food expenses will be about what they are at home, $25 to $30 a week. If you stay in motels and eat all your meals in restaurants they will cost at least $5 per person per day: breakfast $1, lunch $1.50, dinner $2.50 or more. This would be $35 a week per person, or $140 for a family of four. Then there is the compromise: a low-cost picnic lunch on a touring vacation, or an occasional restaurant meal while you are camping. Don't forget the older children are inclined to eat more than just a half-portion, and it is best to make the same food allowance for them as for adults.

In considering the cost of accommodations, camping will be almost negligible—except for $300 or more worth of camping equipment, a small investment if you use it over a period of years. Figure such small expenses as camping fees, fuel for stove and lantern, and laundry at $1 a day. Stopping at motels, a family of four does very well indeed to find suitable facilities for $8 a night. Better allow $10 and expect some nights at $12. For hotels with summer family rates (children and parking free), figure $10. If you're camping, consider the possibility of an occasional motel or hotel night. Cottages and cabins come in a great range of prices, but you can figure about $65 a week in a national or state park, $90 at the seaside or mountains. A resort vacation will cost a family of four anywhere from $25 a day at a modest spot to $35 or $40 a day at a more luxurious type resort. This includes, not only room and meals, but entertainment, sports, and children's activities.

On the touring vacation you have to allow for admissions and amusements. If saving is a necessity, lean heavily on the free ones. You can map out a delightful tour with negligible sightseeing expenses. Too few people realize that museums, as an institution, have undergone a revolution, at long last blown out dust and cobwebs. Today's typical museum, whether indoors or outdoors, is a revitalized place offering fun and learning, with techniques borrowed from the theatre, art gallery, architect, industrial designer and even television.

There are many worth while commercial attractions, of course, private operations and collections that represent creative initiative, showmanship and heavy investment. But be selective. Don't fall for the endless chain of big billboards proclaiming the greatest show on earth (anyway, that's the circus!). Visit such places as caverns, historic shrines and scenic attractions because they really interest you and your family. Know the cost beforehand so you will not be surprised, nor your children disappointed, should you suddenly discover the admission is more than you can afford. Allow ample time to enjoy fully every place you visit—you can't get the most out of any attraction when you are in a hurry. Allow about $2 a day per person for sight-seeing.

Food, lodgings, and car operation account for almost 80 per cent of the vacation budget, but don't lose sight of the lesser items that make up the remainder, including little items like postal cards, camera film, and souvenirs.

You can figure about $100 a week for a family of four on a camping vacation; $225 if you are traveling the motel route, $280 at a resort hotel. For your own protection, add on 10 or 15 per cent for incidentals and emergencies. Should you need a new tire and tube, for instance, you'll have to dig down for $25.

Along with developing your budget, try to determine a sensible distance to travel. If you have a two-week vacation, don't try to stretch it into a trip that should take three weeks. It doesn't make much sense for anyone who works eight hours a day in office or shop to spend more than eight hours behind the wheel of his car on vacation. In planning, try to provide for less, rather than more, daily driving time. Add up your vacation time and money. If you have four weeks available and the funds to match it, then you can consider crossing the continent. If not, lower your sights and enjoy the country closer to home.

Men, there is one sure way to save money—and keep your wife happy. Let her handle the budget and the wallet. Women know how to get the full value out of a dollar. Men may be experts at earning money, but the ladies have more experience in spending it. Ever watched them save pennies at the supermarket? They really know how, and on a vacation trip they can contrive to stretch dollars.

Women are especially sensible in matters relating to tipping, fair but

not foolish. And tipping is probably the biggest headache the vacationer has to face. It will always be with us, as long as customers want
to express their appreciation for service or hope to buy a little extra.
Even where tipping is forbidden, or written into the check, someone
always persists in tipping and before you know it the bars are down.

There is no reason to be on the defensive about tipping. You don't
have to tip anybody anywhere anything. You do so only because you
want to, in appreciation for service well rendered. When you pay your
hotel bill, your restaurant check, your night-club bill, or your taxi fare,
you have met your obligation. You do not owe a penny more, and you
do not have to pay another penny to leave feeling as expansive as the
big tipper.

And speaking of high class restaurants and night spots, here is an
inside tip: if the total is tallied in pencil and not on the cash register,
double check it—just for luck, shall we say.

Should I, you ask, tip 10 or 15 per cent? The standard has risen, to
be sure, but let the quality of service, rather than any arbitrary standard, determine the amount of your tip. If you're obliged to wait half
an hour for a menu or a glass of water, if the food is thrown at you,
if the taxi driver is impertinent or the bell boy behaves officiously, use
your judgment and tip accordingly. Considering that tips constitute a
large portion of their income, these people ought to be courteous. Most
of them are, and you should be fair with them.

Don't think of a big tip as the mark of a good traveler. If you're
traveling on an expense account, that is one thing. It doesn't come out
of your pocket—all you do is sign the check and forget about it. Without tax deductions or an expense account? In that case, avoid going
overboard. The people who depend on tips know the difference between
business travelers and vacationing families. How generous can they
be on their trips? Quite likely, less than extravagant.

And don't be coerced by the shiny quarter the hatcheck girl displays
on the handy tray; she doesn't get that much from everyone.

13

Souvenirs that Count

There probably isn't a man, woman, or child in the United States who
at some time hasn't acquired a souvenir away from home. It may have

been a 10¢ trinket. Or a $2000 fur coat. But the odds are that if you made a trip you purchased something as a memento to keep for yourself or as a gift for someone else. Souvenir shopping is part of everybody's trip. And yet the wonder is that so much money is invested in doodads, imitation knickknacks, and assorted low-grade merchandise which could just as well be purchased at home—if one really wanted them.

Without criticizing the customers of those acre-wide trinket counters, or the manufacturers and merchants who purvey them, there ought to be, there must be, a better way. The well-financed traveler is at a decided advantage, of course. He is able to visit better shops, to consider costlier merchandise; whether he chooses intelligently is another matter, but at least the economic factor is not as pressing with him as with the rest of us. For that very reason—that one has less money to spend, and precious little to waste—the average citizen ought to be a selective, discriminating shopper rather than a willing victim at the junk counters.

Shopping wisely can be pleasant, too, adding a new perspective to travel, enabling you to acquire items of intrinsic value for your home or as presents for friends. Inevitably, the thoughtful shopper grows interested in local products and handicrafts. No longer is he satisfied with anything short of authenticity; he appreciates the craftsman's skill and its relationship to the traditions of the region. Shopping for worthwhile souvenirs need not be costly either, for even the best craft shops cater to the moderate-price market as well as the luxury field.

One area where you can combine touring with shopping for useful, sensibly priced handicrafts is the Southern Highlands—Virginia, Tennessee, Kentucky, Carolinas, West Virginia, and Georgia. The opportunity to watch them made is an attraction of the mountains, an expression of the people in the same sense that natural scenery is an expression of the land. The gentle skills would likely be lost and traditions forgotten were it not for such shops and schools as Allanstand and Biltmore Industries in Asheville, Pi Beta Phi in Gatlinburg, and the other member shops of the Southern Highlanders Handicraft Guild, a nonprofit group which has built a co-operative spirit among the widely scattered craftsmen. It endeavors to establish fair prices for workmanship, to improve quality, and to provide centers where members can display and sell their wares. At their shops in the Blue Ridge and Smoky Mountains craftsmen work on textiles, wood carving, ornamental iron, silver, pottery, and handmade furniture. Every July members of the Guild converge on Gatlinburg, Tennessee, for the five-

The craftsman at work: Douglas J. Ferguson, the potter of Pigeon Forge, Tennessee.

day Craftsman's Fair, setting up their looms, benches, and wheels, working in full view at the Civic Auditorium.

What makes a souvenir worth buying? "The most important consideration," replies Douglas J. Ferguson, a real artisan of the Pigeon Forge Pottery near Gatlinburg, "is that it should represent the area. It should be made by a craftsman and identified with a hallmark—and I don't mean 'Made in Japan.' Significant craft items will have their own hallmark and the discriminating buyer should hesitate if he doesn't see it."

Doesn't one usually pay more for a label or hallmark? "No," according to Doug Ferguson. "A craftsman will always be more concerned with his reputation and the quality of his work than with the price he receives. And if a product is made with distinction, using native materials and expressing the spirit of an area, then it justifies the purchaser's consideration. The fact of craftsmanship, rather than machine construction, enhances value many times. Yet here in the Highlands a number of artistic items can be purchased for one fourth or one fifth of the price they bring in the large cities."

The Pigeon Forge Pottery produces ingenious, useful items, many moderately priced. And long after one's visit they recall to mind the best of the Great Smoky Mountains.

The Indians of the Southwest produce another wonderful type of craft souvenir in their rugs, silver, pottery, and mounted gems. The Hopi, Navaho, Apache, and Pueblo Indians, who are among the most creative artisans in the history of the world, inherit their touch from prehistoric forebears, the Basket Makers of the cliffs and mesas. They have always produced objects of beauty and utility with remarkably few, primitive tools. Even today, many a fine silversmith uses an old piece of railroad rail for his anvil. Pottery is fashioned without benefit of a potter's wheel; skill and patience are not wanting, particularly in such artists as Maria of San Ildefonso, famous the world over for her polished black pottery. Scarcely anywhere can one purchase more hours of human labor for a dollar than a Navaho rug, quite apart from beauty and utility. Today, when the Indian can buy most of what he needs, the hand products are made for non-Indian buyers— tourists—but does this make the material any less authentic? Scarcely, for the old concha belts, bracelets, rings, necklaces, and rugs of 50 or 75 years ago, on display at historic museums, are remarkably similar to, though a little heavier, than those made now. Maintaining standards of quality, however, is an unending struggle. The tourist market is glutted with imitations made of modern synthetics and even some Indians merchandise phony curios.

The Indian trader, Fred Thompson, displays Indian rugs at the Santo Domingo Trading Post, New Mexico. An authentic trading post is one of the best places for shopping and sight-seeing in the Indian country of the Southwest.

An authentic Indian trading post usually is a good place to shop, as well as to spend a leisurely hour or two observing the Indians. The trading post is their "general store," where Indians barter with the white trader, pawn and redeem jewelry, buy groceries and clothing, meet their old cronies sometimes after lonely sheepherding on a vast reservation. One of the most accessible and engaging trading posts is operated by Fred Thompson at Santo Domingo Pueblo, midway between Santa Fe and Albuquerque. Trader Fred, formerly an insurance salesman in Rochester, New York, took to western ways and settled happily on the Domingo reservation. Here are his shopping suggestions, which apply, not only to the Indian Country, but to souvenir shopping everywhere:

"It is extremely important to purchase from a reputable place. The average citizen would not dare buy anything of value on a street corner in his home town, yet he will on a vacation—and find out later he has been stung. This advice applies to buying from an Indian in India, a Mexican in Mexico, an Indian in this country, even here in Santo Domingo Pueblo.

"For some reason, people seem to lose their good sense when they trade with an Indian. Little do they realize the 'poor fellow' makes a living by kidding the public. Some of our Indians have a great little business buying imitation ten-cent-store jewelry and palming it off on tourists as being real. And anybody who thinks he can outbargain an Indian learns he is wrong. These people are shrewd merchants, who will not sell anything for less than it is worth.

Craft items, glassware to furniture, are sold at Williamsburg as a useful type of souvenir. The Craft House presents an introduction to colonial furniture and furnishings.

"Another point: if a person sees something he likes at a reputable place and can afford it, he ought to buy it without worrying whether he can save a few cents somewhere else. A traveler's time should be too valuable to spend in pricing items. It usually works out that the price is higher at the next place and then it is too late to turn around and head back. If he does return, the object already may be sold; if you admired it, chances are someone else will, too."

Inquire from a reliable source, such as a chamber of commerce or a motel operator, to learn where you can get the widest selection and the best buy. This way you get the opinion of someone who does not get a commission or have an interest in a store. Above all, the reputable dealer with an established business must give fair value, count on repeat business and recommendations. A street peddler is interested only in the spot sale. Ask yourself, "Can this item be returned for refund? Will I be able to contact the seller later?"

Another New Mexican, John Kennedy, of Gallup, is probably the biggest wholesaler in the Indian country. John spent part of his boyhood at Chinle, Arizona, near Canyon de Chelly, when his father was the Indian trader there; later he became the trader at Zuni Pueblo, noted for its silverwork, and now he is one of the leading officials of the Gallup Intertribal Ceremonial. To businessmen like John Kennedy the machine-made goods are a monstrous headache.

"The most distressing thing," he feels, "is that much of their merchandise is tagged 'Indian Style,' 'Indian Design' or some such tricky catchword. The buying public seems only to see the word 'Indian' and buys the cheap product. It is often difficult for a layman to understand that a low-priced product cannot be made from precious metal, semiprecious stone and hand labor.

"We succeeded in getting a state law passed requiring that all manufactured items be so designated, but the law has been tied up by various injunctions for over a year. The manufacturers can provide a much stronger lobby than a group of us crazy Indian traders!"

If you want to buy the real thing, watch out for those tricky labels, which are cleverly within the framework of a federal law against selling imitations labeled as Indian made. The law provides a $2000 fine and six months' imprisonment for violations. The buyer has the right to ask for a bill of sale with certification of authenticity; if you have any questions about a purchase or believe you have been duped, advise the Arts and Crafts Board, Department of the Interior, Washington 25, D.C.

Other types of distinctive souvenirs worth the effort and money to acquire:

Foodstuffs: New England maple syrup, Wisconsin and Minnesota cheese, Louisiana canned creole foods, Virginia and Tennessee country ham, Pennsylvania Dutch sausage, California brandied figs. They recall the pleasures of your trip every time you taste them; usually you can have them sent as gifts, rather than having to tote them along.

Furniture: Craft items such as those sold at colonial Williamsburg enhance gracious living and bring the flavor of places you admire into your home.

Paintings: Excellent original oils and water colors, often at low cost, are sold at villages along the Maine coast, New Orleans, San Francisco, the Southwest.

Pipestone: A curious, though understandable, circumstance: for 300 years the American Plain Indians obtained pipes of peace from the sacred, storied quarries at Pipestone, Minnesota. Today, use of the pipestone is reserved by law to the Indians, quarried by them under special permit from the Interior Department, and fashioned into attractive souvenirs.

Driftwood: The price is free along sandy beaches. Take it home for use in floral arrangements, on your mantel, or fashion your own mobile.

14

Fifteen Favorite Vacations
Trips, Places, Events

Tour No. 1
St. Lawrence Seaway and Eastern Canada

Watching large ocean going vessels pass through the locks of the St. Lawrence Seaway on their course between the Atlantic Ocean and the Great Lakes evokes that vicarious sense of travel to distant places. For these ships, loaded with iron ore, coal, grain, pulpwood—and now with passengers—link the inland sea with the corners of the globe. But don't stop there. From the Seaway, you can travel into Canada, the closest thing to Europe without a transatlantic crossing.

Europeans who view with disdain the U. S. version of antiquity are more respectful in this section of Canada. Not only was it established early in the seventeenth century but in many ways it looks, feels, and

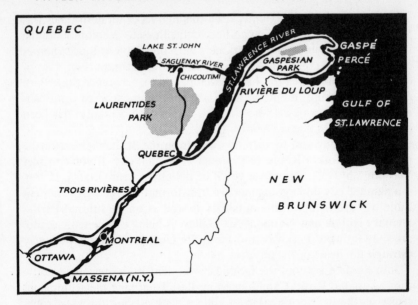

sounds European. This is not to call it an imitation or substitute, but all you need is your own car—without passport, tipping guide, travel agent's itinerary, airline or steamship tickets. And while a European vacation would likely cost a couple a minimum of $1500, you can spend a satisfying week or ten days in Canada for less than $300.

Best place to start your Seaway-to-Canada trip is at Massena, New York, site of the most spectacular link in the entire Seaway between Montreal and Lake Erie. If you are coming from the West, follow Route 37, or Route 2 on the Canadian side, passing attractive regions like the Thousand Islands. From the South, stop at Cooperstown on Otsego Lake, on Route 80, to see the Baseball and Farmers Museums.

When you arrive at Massena, call first at Seaway headquarters, on Andrews Street, for maps and literature. A local bus company operates guided trips three times daily ($1.50, children 75¢) or you can drive your car and follow the markers to the 10-mile Wiley-Dondero Ship Channel and the towering Eisenhower and Snell Locks, which raise and lower vessels 90 feet. Five years ago this area was farmland, but during the course of the billion dollar Seaway project the International Rapids and 38 million yards of rock and clay were eliminated, the meandering St. Lawrence transformed into a lake at this point. From four overlooks you can watch the ships; they can now navigate the full 2,430 miles between the Atlantic and Duluth, Minnesota, at the western limit of the Great Lakes.

Massena, a quiet community until this marvel of modern times was thrust in its midst, is still expanding its facilities to accommodate the influx of businessmen and vacationers with new motels, tourist homes and a new hotel ($8–$15). Advance reservations are important. Campers: an entire new area has been developed in St. Lawrence State Park on Barnhart Island; the River and Lake both offer excellent trout fishing. For golfers, a new 18-hole course (greens fee, $3 daily) has been opened by the Massena Country Club.

Continue your tour by turning away from the St. Lawrence, for the present, and follow Route 16 to Canada's capital city. If you consider Washington, D.C., attractive, you'll be delighted with Ottawa. It, too, is a planned city undergoing modern transformation. New Government buildings are rising on the outskirts as well as on traditional Parliamentary Hill. A new National Art Gallery is being completed; so, too, are the Gatineau Parkway and Park, the Queensway, an expressway through the heart of the city.

Join the free tours of the Gothic Parliament Buildings, guarded by the red-coated Royal Canadian Mounties. Then take the scenic boat cruise on the Rideau Canal ($1, children 50¢), a beautiful water route through the city and its parks, first dug as an avenue of escape for British gunboats during the War of 1812. Other major attractions: the National Museum of Canada and the National Gallery of Art; the Royal Canadian Mint, and the Royal Canadian Mounted Police Barracks, at Rockcliffe, where good fellows like Sergeant Preston get their start. Dine at the Café Champlain on Bate Island.

From Ottawa, cross into Quebec Province and drive to cosmopolitan Montreal, the second largest French city in the world and proud of it. Old places it has, like the Place Royale, center of the original settlement in 1642; Chateau de Ramezay, built in 1705, and Notre Dame church; but its charm, as in cities like New Orleans and San Francisco, is in the spirit as much as the substance. Montreal has many fine eating places. The Tour Eiffel, typically French, is one; Drury's venerable English Inn another.

The farther north you travel along the St. Lawrence River the less you hear English spoken, the more you feel you are on foreign soil. At Quebec you reach the fountainhead of la Nouvelle France, a walled city founded in 1608 by Champlain, then the starting point for explorations to the Great Lakes, the Mississippi, and as far west as the Rockies. Quebec's rocky precipice sits above the St. Lawrence, its

Chatting with a red-coated Mountie at Parliament Hill, Ottawa. In the background is the Gothic Peace Tower.

Little changed after four centuries, the village of Percé, at the eastern end of the Gaspé Peninsula, faces wooded Bonaventure Island, a bird sanctuary, and the open sea.

narrow streets twisting and winding upwards. Follow the walking tour to points of interest like the Citadel, where Roosevelt and Churchill stayed during their Quebec conference in World War II; Battlefields Park, where Wolfe defeated Montcalm; the seventeenth-century Parliament Buildings, and Dufferin Terrace, the boardwalk promenade. Dine at the Fleur de Lys in the Château Laurier Hotel.

The cities are only the starting point of Canadian vacationing. Beyond them lie the cantons, the townships, woods and lakes, unhurried, little changing, friendly—and inexpensive.

You can drive East to the Gaspé Peninsula, where the villages, the countryside, the language are unmistakably French. And a $20 million road building program has overcome once hazardous cliff-side driving and rough gravel surface. Route 6 begins at Ste. Flavie on the St. Lawrence, 205 miles northeast of Quebec. Drive around the north coast to the village of Gaspé, the site of Cartier's landfall four centuries ago, then along the sandy beaches of the south coast.

Explore the Gaspé interior, too. The Gaspesian Park, 1300 square miles of woodland, has facilities for camping, or stay at attractive Mont Albert Inn ($3.50).

In another direction from Quebec, you can drive due north on a new road (Routes 54 and 54B) into and beyond the Laurentides Park, one of the finest in Canada's growing national and provincial park system—which Americans know too little about. Laurentides, for instance, is larger than Yellowstone; it contains 1,500 lakes, mountains rising to 4,000 feet. There are campgrounds and three inns, including Le Relais ($5) on the shores of beautiful Lac Jacques Cartier. North of the Park you are on the Saguenay River, a beautiful tributary of the St. Lawrence. While you're in this area, try to combine a boat trip with your motoring—a delightful relief from the wheel. Highly recommended: four-hour cruise from Tadoussac to Bagotville ($6 for car; $3.05 per passenger, half-fare for children).

Tour No. 2
New England Seacoast

New England's distances are short—it would take 200 tiny Rhode Islands to fill Texas. And in a hurry you could cover the 330 miles from New York to Portland, Maine, in about seven hours. But slow down, give the turnpikes a rest en route, at least long enough for you to touch New England's history, traditional architecture and scenery.

The most popular season is summer, when vacationers throng the beach resorts. Delay your trip until after Labor Day and you should save about 15 to 20 per cent in cost and find the best accommodations readily available. Another choice period is mid-October, when you can enjoy the contrast of the sea and the changing autumn foliage inland. Two people can spend a week's vacation touring the New England Coast for about $180, a family of four for $250.

Starting from New York, head north on the new 15-mile section of the New York Thruway, directly to the Connecticut Turnpike at the state border. Make your first stop—especially if you're traveling with youngsters—Mystic Seaport (use Groton Interchange from the Turnpike), a restoration of a Nineteenth Century seafaring village on the banks of the Mystic River.

Grounds and buildings are open all year (9–5, $1.50, children 50¢); once this very site was dotted with bustling shipyards and was home port of noted captains. Today cobblestoned Seaport Street is a picture book scene, its inshore side lined with old shops and homes, its wharf

Open House at Newport—This pleasant summer "cottage," built by Cornelius Vanderbilt in 1895, is now open to the public, opulence and all, from May through October. It overlooks Cliff Walk.

filled with 50-odd boats and ships. Youngsters love to board the wooden whaler "Charles W. Morgan." This is a living, active port. You will find craftsmen at work in their lofts—shipsmith, figurehead carver, modelmaker. Picnic tables are available in summer or you can lunch at the Galley.

When you enter Rhode Island, follow Routes 1 and 138, then take a pleasant one-hour voyage across Narragansett Bay from Jamestown to Newport, on a fast new diesel-powered ferry. After generations as the sanctuary of high society at leisure, Newport's exclusive door is open. You can swim at the seaside and tour summer palaces of another era.

The showplace is the Breakers, the 70-room Vanderbilt mansion on Ochre Point, now leased to the Newport Preservation Society (open daily 10–5, to 9 in summer; $1.60, children 60¢). Within this mass of Italian Renaissance marble and alabaster are rooms with 45 foot ceilings, detailed wood carvings, statuary and mammoth loggias overlooking the Ocean. Belcourt, another elaborate mansion (10–5, $1.60, children 60¢), faces Bailey's Beach—still the private retreat of the elite. Belcourt houses treasures of antique furnishings dating to the Twelfth Century.

You can stay at a converted mansion, too: Ocean Mansion ($10 double), overlooking the clustered yachts in Newport Harbor and Narragansett Bay. As for eating, be sure to try the White Horse Tavern, which first opened its doors in 1687 and was recently restored to serve Rhode Island specialties like johnnycakes and chowder.

The White Horse represents Newport's early career as a seaport rivaling New York and Boston. Around Washington Square you will see hundreds of old homes and public buildings recalling that day, including Touro Synagogue, a National Historic Site, the oldest synagogue in America (1763) and a beautiful colonial house of worship.

This area of New England is the happy hunting ground of anti-

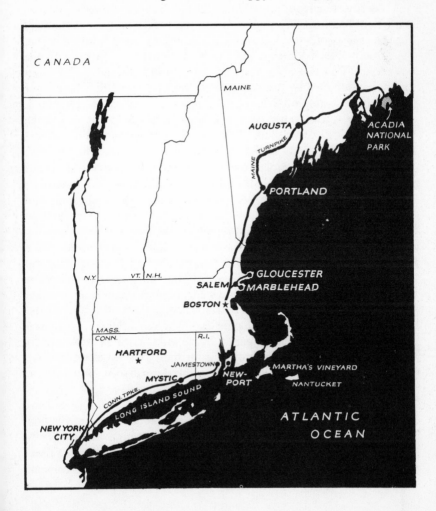

quarians and history-minded of all ages; you arrive at the core in the small ancient area of downtown Boston called the "Old City." The narrow, winding streets on the 1¼ mile "Freedom Trail" are lined with shrines and quiet reminders of patriotic doings two centuries ago.

First, pick up a copy of the Visitor's Guide at the Boston Visitor's Bureau, 80 Federal Street. Then start at Boston Common, created as a community cow pasture in 1634. Follow the arrows to points of interest like the Granary Burying Ground, where John Hancock, Samuel Adams and Paul Revere are buried; the Old State House, facing the Boston Massacre scene; Faneuil (pronounced Fan'l) Hall, the "Cradle of Liberty" where revolutionary meetings were held.

A nearby luncheon stop: Union Oyster House, for seafood in a century-old setting. Then continue on the Freedom Trail to the Paul Revere House, oldest home in Boston, and Old North Church, where the lantern was held from the tower to signal Paul Revere. While downtown, visit the State House, still wearing the handsome front and dome designed by Bulfinch in 1795, and Beacon Hill, where other architectural examples of that period are preserved in private homes.

Boston is a children's city, too. Your youngsters will enjoy the Franklin Park Zoo, Museum of Science, Children's Museum and perhaps best of all the "U. S. S. Constitution" (conducted tours 9:30–4, free). Direct budding scholars across the Charles River to visit Harvard University and Massachusetts Institute of Technology at Cambridge.

Along the Massachusetts north shore are the fishing, shipping and yachting centers of Marblehead, Salem and Gloucester. Stop at least in Salem, probably known most widely as the scene of the notorious witch hunts of the 17th Century, but which deserves remembrance for finer hours. At the waterfront, for example, Salem National Historic Site (9–5, free) preserves the heart of the old seaport; merchant princes ushered in the first golden age of American foreign trade when they sent ships from here on trade routes the world over. At the customs house you can see the pine desk where Nathaniel Hawthorne spent three years as a bookkeeper. In his later writings he described this and other places still standing. Tour the House of Seven Gables (10–5, 75¢, children 30¢), complete, as he described it, down to the secret stairway.

To follow the story of the sea, visit the Peabody Museum (9–5, Sunday 2–5, free), a wonderful collection of nautical paintings, navigation instruments, models of whaling vessels—it was begun by a group of sea captains in 1799. Another fine Salem museum, the Essex House (Tuesday–Saturday 9–4:30, Sunday 2–5, free) displays Federal and colonial period furniture, portraits, costumes, documents.

In terms of natural scenery, the finest of the New England Coast, and probably of the entire Atlantic shoreline, is at Acadia National Park (Route 3 from the terminus of the Maine Turnpike at Augusta). The Park occupies 29 surf-splashed granite cliffs crowned with a cool mountain forest. It was discovered by Champlain in 1604 and settled briefly by the French. Once it was a fashionable summering place but in 1916 it became the first national park east of the Mississippi.

There are many places in Acadia for swimming and fishing, both fresh water and salt water. The National Park Service conducts a full program of nature walks, hikes and evening campfires. By all means join the Naturalist Sea Cruise ($2.50, children under 12, $1.25), probing the scenic highlights from the waters of Frenchman Bay. When you stop at Cadillac Mountain, you will see magnificent vistas of the Ocean in one direction, the land to distant Mount Katahdin in the other.

Only campers are permitted to sleep in the Park, and space is in such demand that you are limited to 14 days. Accommodations are available (motel rooms average $14 double) in adjoining resort communities of Bar Harbor, Northeast Harbor, Southwest Harbor and Winter Harbor. Reservations are advisable during July and August.

Tour No. 3

Washington—The Capital and Gateway to the Civil War

The Nation's Capital is visited yearly by six million Americans and many from other countries. This is all to the good, for Washington is an active, living representation of democracy. But be sure to visit it as such, and not simply as an arrangement of monuments and marble, impressive though they may be.

When you come to Washington, broaden your sights. See the usual, popular attractions, but explore others, too. Look for the new buildings and history-making sites of the '60's. Find the areas of interest to you *outside* the Government. Sense Washington as a city with a distinct personality of its own, as well as a political entity that belongs to all America. Take advantage of your nearness to Virginia, Maryland and West Virginia—within three hours drive are mountains, ocean, history. And as the Civil War Centennial comes into focus, consider Washington as the gateway to the scenes of dramatic action from first Manassas to Appomattox.

First, the seasons. Springtime is finest. The lovely Japanese cherry blossoms around the Tidal Basin emerge in delicate pink and white bloom early in April. Spring is most crowded; be sure you have reservations. Summer, it must be admitted, has its shortcomings. It can be hot, but during the Summer Jubilee, June 15 to Labor Day, hotels offer family rates and free parking to compensate for the climate. Many motels and a few hotels have swimming pools. Sheraton-Park, for instance, on 16 landscaped acres uptown, charges $12 double, children under 14 free. Autumn is an excellent season to visit Washington: mild, dry weather, fewer crowds on Government building tours, and beautiful foliage in the nearby mountains.

Plan your sightseeing to get the most out of your time in a given section. For instance, block out a full day at Capitol Hill. Start by making your presence known at the office of your senator or congressman; his staff members may have suggestions for you. From the Senate Office Building, ride the little underground railroad to the Capitol Building. Best way to explore these hallowed halls: a guided, 40-minute sightseeing tour (25¢, children free). You may be in time to see Congress in session or a Committee hearing underway—these show the legislative process in action. Have lunch at the new Senate Office Building cafeteria, of bean soup, a time honored Congressional dish, and the famous Senate rum pie (served Wednesdays). After lunch, visit the buildings nearby—first to watch the U. S. Supreme Court in session (Monday to Thursday, noon to 4 P.M.), then the Library of Congress, the U. S. Botanic Garden and the Voice of America studios.

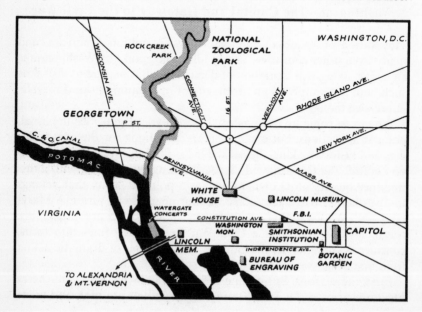

Prepare your own "must-see" list but check the locations and hours carefully. You should include these: White House (Tuesday–Saturday, 10 A.M.–noon); Federal Bureau of Investigation (Monday–Friday, 9:30–4); National Archives (9 A.M. to 10 P.M.), Bureau of Engraving and Printing (8 to 11 A.M. and 12:30 to 2 P.M., Monday–Friday); Smithsonian Institution (9 to 4:30), Washington Monument (9 to 5), and Lincoln Memorial (9 A.M. to 9 P.M., a beautiful spectacle at night). The Lincoln Museum, in the old Ford Theatre where Lincoln was assassinated, is also open until 9 P.M. The newest important Government building is that occupied by the Department of State, now second in size only to the Pentagon.

Washington has excellent cultural attractions, the best known of which is the National Gallery of Art. The Phillips Memorial Gallery presents one of the world's great collections of modern art in an intimate, unmuseum-like setting. Chamber music concerts are presented Sundays at both galleries (also Monday evenings at the Phillips) with admission free. Plan to hear the National Symphony Orchestra and to attend the Arena Stage, which offers orchestra seats at balcony prices ($2)—and fine theatre in the bargain.

An interesting new commercial attraction, the National Historical Wax Museum (75¢, children under 12, 50¢) depicts highlights in American history with life-size figures made of vinyl plastic. Its most recent addition shows the famous four chaplains of World War II aboard the torpedoed troopship Dorchester.

An unusual and popular summer diversion in Washington is the mule-drawn barge trip on the historic C & O Canal (adults, $1; children under 12, 60¢). The trip starts at Georgetown and parallels the Potomac River. It is one of a number of programs conducted by the National Capital Park System. Others: a boat trip on the Anacostia River, walking tours in Rock Creek Park and Theodore Roosevelt Island.

On summer evenings free band concerts are presented at the Watergate, on the Potomac River, by the U. S. Army, Navy and Air Force Bands. You can hear the Marine Band at evening retreats every Friday at the Marine Corps Barracks. At Carter Barron Amphitheatre, in a beautiful setting in Rock Creek Park, Broadway musicals, operettas, ballets and jazz concerts are presented all summer. If you want to splurge on dinner one evening, try the Presidential Room at the famous Mayflower Hotel, the Embassy Room at the Statler, or the Colony.

Drive across the Potomac to Arlington National Cemetery and the Tomb of the Unknowns, then to visit George Washington's home at Mount Vernon (60¢); in this area you should also see Woodlawn, the mansion he had built nearby for his adopted daughter, Nellie Custis (50¢, children under 12 free), and Pohick Church, where he and George Mason were vestrymen.

This region is the heart of Civil War battlegrounds. The Confederates threatened Washington frequently and at one point Jubal Early almost blasted his way into the city. On the other hand, the opposing Capital, Richmond, was only 90 miles away and was the primary objective of the Union forces.

Following are two suggested Civil War itineraries from Washington:

1. Manassas—Harpers Ferry—Antietam—Gettysburg

Drive west on U. S. 29 to Manassas National Battlefield Park, where two important battles were fought. The first, soon after the war began, was a tremendous Southern victory, ending with Union troops and civilian spectators in panicky retreat to Washington. One year later the Confederates, under Lee, Longstreet and Jackson, scored again, opening the way to invade Maryland. From Manassas, follow Route 15 to Harpers Ferry, where the National Monument preserves the site of John Brown's ill-starred raid of 1859. This town, at the confluence of the Potomac and Shenandoah Rivers, changed hands so many times during the War it was completely shattered at the end—and has never recovered. Cross to the Maryland side on U. S. 67 to Antietam National Battlefield Site, scene of one of the bloodiest battles (three generals were lost on each side), in 1862. Neither side won and Lee, who had hoped to invade Pennsylvania, was turned back. Resume Route 15 northward to Gettysburg. Here, on July 1, 1863, began the greatest battle ever fought on the American Continent, involving 170,-000 troops. From many vantage points in the National Battlefield Park you can reconstruct the sequence of action in the three succeeding fateful days and at the National Cemetery you can stand where Abraham Lincoln delivered the Gettysburg Address a few months after the battle. The best way to tour the Battlefield is in company with a licensed guide ($4).

2. Fredericksburg—Richmond—Appomattox

Drive south on Route 350 (Shirley Highway), then U. S. 1 to Fredericksburg. Between 1862–65 four great battles (Fredericksburg, Chancellorsville, Wilderness, Spotsylvania) were fought in and around the town. Start at the National Battlefield Park Museum (25¢) to see

The Canal Clipper *wends its peaceful, mule-powered way along the historic Chesapeake and Ohio Canal, from its starting point in Georgetown; this is one of several popular summer trips conducted by the National Capital Parks.*

the electric map and dioramas. Then drive along Sunken Road, where Longstreet's troops, four deep, fired point blank at charging Union soldiers. Park roads in nearby woods lead to preserved gun pits and trench remains. A high point is the Jackson Shrine at Guinea Station, where Stonewall Jackson died after he was accidentally wounded by one of his own men. Richmond, farther south on U. S. 1, is full of Confederate landmarks: the Confederate Museum, once the White House of Jefferson Davis; the State Capitol, where the Southern Congress met; the Robert E. Lee house, now occupied by the State Historical Society, and Battle Abbey, showing the arms of the Confederacy. East of the city, Richmond National Battlefield Park encompasses the battlegrounds (Seven Pines, Cold Harbor, Fort Harrison, Seven Days) where the Union Army tried but failed to blast its way into the Capital. Finally, Grant was forced to swing south to Petersburg, where he managed to chase the Confederates around Richmond to Appomattox. Drive west on U. S. 60 and 24 to Appomattox Court House National Historic Park, preserving the tiny village where Grant and Lee met and the war ended. The Rebels stacked their guns in defeat, but Grant allowed them to keep their horses.

Tour No. 4
Back to the Farm . . . or to the Ranch

Everybody in the family loves to vacation on the farm. "Yes," you agree, "but where and how do you find a suitable farm to visit unless you have relatives living on one?" You can find the answer in a number of states, perhaps most prominently in central and eastern Pennsylvania, where a group of farm families allied as Denim Blue, Inc., open their homes to guests.

In Western states, instead of visiting a farm, you can stay at a working cattle ranch, join in riding the range, outdoor cooking and back country informality.

Many of the Denim Blue farms, in the beautiful Poconos, the Amish country and along the Susquehanna River, would be ideal as resort locations. Yet their principal attraction is the natural atmosphere of rural living which they offer to city dwellers—at economy rates.

The members of Denim Blue, Inc., are not professional hosts, although they and their farms are required to conform to standards of convenience, comfort, and hospitality. You share with them their surroundings and normal way of life.

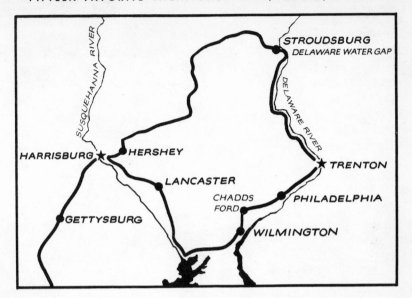

To the children, this means romping with farm youngsters, feeding chickens, pigs, and other animals of the barnyard zoo. Berry picking, hay rides, lake swimming and fishing are part of the fun on a farm, too.

Most of what you eat is home-grown. Such food tastes different! Particularly when you try your own hand at farming and gardening, and pick the fruits of your own labor. Home-baked pies and breads are delectable, but don't worry about your weight—you can work it off.

The Denim Blue farms are close to entertainment and sight-seeing. Those in Chester County are near beautiful Longwood Gardens where operettas are presented during the summer, followed by displays of the colored fountains. The Brandywine Battlefield at Chadds Ford commemorates the site of bitter action and defeat for the Americans under Washington during the Revolutionary War.

Visitors in southeastern Pennsylvania are intrigued by the Amish, the "plain people," adherents to a unique religion who cling to un-mechanical ways. These frugal, efficient farmers, who shun such contrivances as tractors and electricity, wear simple homemade clothing. In the heart of this area Lancaster is a wonderful place to absorb the Pennsylvania Dutch flavor. Have a meal at the Willows, a family dining room on U. S. 30, Lancaster. It runs the full gamut of Pennsylvania Dutch delicacies, from sauerbraten, smoked pork chop, potato pancake, the seven sweet and sours, and shoofly pie.

Plenty to eat for everyone! And the food is home-grown, too, at Meadow Springs, one of the Pennsylvania vacation farms. This one, in Lycoming County, covers 238 acres, with lakes and streams for fishing and swimming, riding horses, and the full complement of barnyard animals.

Several of the farms are in the Poconos, one of the most popular vacation areas of the Northeast, dotted with mountain lakes and waterfalls.

Events, like the Dutch Days, Folk Festival, and Craftsman Show, are held throughout the season. County fairs get underway the first week in August and continue during the fall foliage period of October.

Weekly rates at the farms average $45 to $50 for adults and about half for children. Figure $100 for a couple, about $150 for a family of four. Write Denim Blue, Inc., New Holland, Pennsylvania, for a folder listing individual farms, their facilities and rates. Then pick the farm that sounds most appealing and write directly for full information.

Farm vacationing is rising in popularity throughout the country; a New York hotel agency now publishes a 56-page guide (price, 25¢) covering more than 250 farms in 32 states and Canada. Write Farm Vacations and Holidays, Inc., 500 Fifth Avenue, New York 36, N.Y.

Some Western dude ranches have become as elaborate as resort hotels—and as expensive. Try to stay at what is called a "home ranch," like Walt Lozier's at Cora, Wyoming. It accommodates about 15 guests in cabins or the ranch house. Facilities are not modern—there are still places, believe it or not, without telephone or electricity and where the water is hauled in from the nearest mountain stream—but home-cooked food and atmosphere more than compensate.

Wherever you go, be sure that riding is included in the rate. And do plenty of it. Settle in the stirrups and participate in calf branding, moving the cattle and packing stock salt to the higher ranges. You will see lots of moose, antelope, deer and other wildlife while you're riding. Write Dude Ranchers Association, Billings, Montana.

Tour No. 5

Blue Ridge Parkway and Mountains

Vacationers could ask for no more in a road than what they experience on the Blue Ridge Parkway. Its only purpose is recreation for the man behind the wheel and his family.

The Parkway is a road, but more than a road. It is a link between

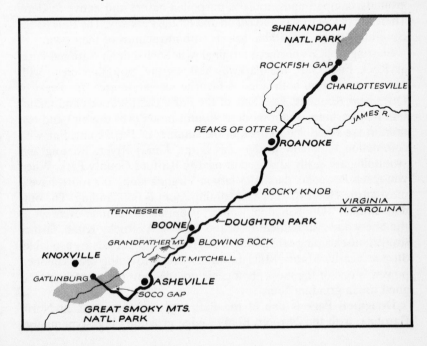

two national parks, Shenandoah and the Great Smokies; an elongated park in its own right, and a lookout post from which to view a way of life quickly vanishing—the isolation of the traditional mountaineer. The Parkway is a mountaintop garden, in bloom from spring to the end of summer, alternately with dogwood, pink and flame azalea, purple rhododendron, mountain laurel, and a complexion of wild-flowers; all this followed by a blaze of autumnal color.

Even as a road the Parkway represents a new concept, designed, not as an expressway, but as a leisurely touring route. John D. Rockefeller, Jr., with all his millions, finds this one of his favorite trips. Yet you and he own equal shares of this national park area. A couple can enjoy a three-day tour through the region for less than $50 or a week's stay for under $125. A family of four can manage three days for $75, a week for $200, with something left over.

In time the Parkway will cover nearly 500 miles; it is now about three-fourths complete, with federal and state roads forming connecting links between the gaps. It is completely free of billboards and commercial traffic.

Instead, you will find convenient parking overlooks, 3000 feet and higher, for observing wide valleys, clusters of mountains, and low-lands. At intervals along the Parkway are recreation areas with picnic grounds, campgrounds, trails to unspoiled nature and native folklore. There are places to stay and eat on and off the Parkway. The Blue Ridge communities are hospitable resorts with attractions of their own.

Starting from its northern terminal with Shenandoah National Park, at Rock Fish Gap, the Parkway follows the mountain crest, with sweeping views on both sides. A favorite recreation area, the Peaks of Otter near Roanoke, has some of the finest campgrounds and mountain trout fishing; and a modern 40-unit motel ($10 double) and restaurant are scheduled to open in the summer of 1960, coinciding with completion of a new bridge across the James River. Boating and swimming are easily arranged at nearby Bedford County Park. When you reach Roanoke, the major city in Virginia along the route, have a meal at the Hotel Roanoke; its dining room is outstanding. The outdoor drama, "Thy Kingdom Come," is presented summer evenings at the Sherwood Amphitheatre (tickets $2–$3). At Rocky Knob, farther south, housekeeping cabins ($6 per day) and campgrounds are available. Stop at nearby Mabry Mill: its waterwheel, providing old-fashioned power, is one of the most photogenic points—and the power is put to good use in grinding flour.

Doughton Park is one of the Parkway's notable areas in North Carolina, with the 24-room Bluffs Lodge providing high-type motor-

Mabry Mill, a vestige of the pioneer past, a highlight along the Blue Ridge Parkway. The turning waterwheel still provides old-fashioned power.

court accommodations ($7–$8 double), and 20 miles of trail through laurel, azalea and other mountain flowers to places like Wildcat Rock overlooking a pioneer cabin in a deep, isolated valley. At Boone, six miles off the Parkway, Kermit Hunter's outdoor drama, *Horn in the West,* is presented from late June through August (tickets $2–$3). Near Blowing Rock the Moses H. Cone Memorial Park, 3600-acre former estate of the "Blue Denim King" of Greensboro, N.C., has been incorporated in the Parkway and the manor house converted to a craft center, operated by the Southern Highlands Handicraft Guild. If you are looking for an unusual and low-cost resort, Pinnacle Inn at Banner Elk, west of the Parkway, may be the answer. It is a conversion of Lees-McRae College to a summer hotel, largely staffed by students. Rates begin at $6.50 a day, American plan. The food comes from the inn's own farms.

Grandfather Mountain (elevation 5900 feet), near Linville, is not on the Parkway, but a road leads to its mile-high swinging bridge (admission, 50¢). Linville Falls was thought so beautiful by John D. Rockefeller, Jr., that he bought it and presented it to the Parkway. Farther south a state road leads to Mount Mitchell State Park and the summit of the highest peak in eastern America (6680 feet). The Parkway continues to the resort city of Asheville. Here the Biltmore House ($2.40, children $1.40) is one of the country's great mansions, a relic of another day, surrounded by formal and informal gardens and a 12,000 acre estate. Literary landmarks: the Thomas Wolfe home (50¢) and Riverside Cemetery, where Wolfe and O. Henry are buried. Drive west through the Cherokee Reservation, where the Indians have built and operate a fine motor court, Boundary Tree ($7–$10 double). Summer evenings the Cherokees are featured performers in "Unto These Hills," an outdoor drama (tickets $1.50–$3). Ask the directions to Sunset Farms, a lovely country dining place, serving family-style meals of trout, ham, chicken, and all the trimmings. Then drive on to the terminal of the Parkway at Soco Gap, the gateway to the Great Smokies.

Tour No. 6
Gold Fever in Dahlonega

Here is a real do-it-yourself vacation—panning for gold at the scene of the country's first gold rush. A very pleasant scene too, at Dahlonega, in the northern Georgia foothills, where the gold strike started back in 1828. These fields yielded $60 million worth of gold and were so productive a federal mint was established at Dahlonega—although 20 years later the mint assayer was forced to plead with the miners not to follow the brighter trail to California. "There's gold in them thar hills," he insisted, pointing to Dahlonega's environs, but they did not heed him.

If you cannot make it to Dahlonega, there are other places in the country where you can try your hand at digging for gold or for other precious minerals. Once you start rockhounding it grows into a pleasant, sometimes profitable hobby, which is easily combined with travel. Youngsters like to "rockhound," too, and some families make a practice of collecting at least one mineral as a memento of every state they visit. When you get serious about digging and collecting precious and semi-precious stones, a good book to have is the Gem Hunter's Guide by Russell P. MacFall. Just remember this simple rule: take what you need and leave some for the next fellow. Denuding mineral grounds is the sure way to ruin a fast-growing hobby.

Dahlonega is no ghost town, but a thriving community of 2500 population, in a scenic mountain setting at the edge of Chattahoochee

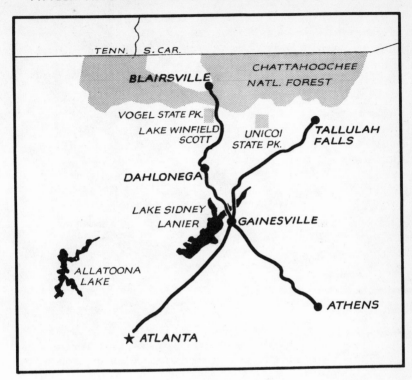

National Forest. Though it costs more than the market price to mine gold commercially, vacationers delight in panning. Nobody gets rich but you should at least find enough gold worth carrying home as souvenirs, if not to sell. Two people can spend a week vacationing here for $125, possibly less, four in a family for under $200; with everybody panning, you may even recoup some of it!

A number of convenient points are recommended for panning. The handiest, the Gold Museum, at the foot of Crown Mountain, is operated by the chamber of commerce on a non-profit basis. It is probably the only museum in the world with a dirt floor and a stream of gold running through it. For 50¢ you get panning instructions from an expert and free use of the museum sluice box and the nearby mining gulches. Or you can pan at Auraria, first boom town and first ghost town, where you pay a dollar for the entire day with success assured— well, almost. And the American Legion has property on which anybody can pan free.

Panning isn't difficult. All it takes is practice and patience. Fill the pan three fourths full of panning dirt, then wash out all the dirt, clay,

The best stream in Dahlonega, where good luck is almost guaranteed and everybody turns to gold panning with a vengeance.

trash, and rocks. If anything is left in the form of tiny glittering grains, you have come upon pure gold. If nothing is left, keep panning.

At the museum, visitors see countless complicated gadgets used for extracting gold from the earth, as well as gold specimens in varied forms—rock, dust, nuggets, and coins minted at Dahlonega. A hiking trail starts from the museum across the old mining country to the John C. Calhoun Mine, owned by the famous South Carolina senator; the Barlow Mine, in which U. S. Grant reportedly was a stockholder; and the Consolidated Mine, in which millions were invested for a disappointingly low return.

Dahlonega's hotel and motel are moderately priced ($5–$7 double), and even the local people come to the Smith House for its family-style dinners ($1.29 during the week; $1.55 on Sunday). Three nearby state parks, Vogel, Unicoi and Amicalola, provide cabin accommodations; so does the new Lake Winfield Scott Recreation Area (weekly rates, $40–$85). There is plenty of pleasant, cool Blue Ridge country for touring, complete with fishing streams and waterfalls.

Big doings Saturday nights during the summer are the outdoor square dances in Valeria Sykes Park on Crown Mountain. The year's main event, however, is Gold Rush Day in October. It begins at 10 A.M. with a man on horseback riding into the square announcing the discovery of gold. From then on the day is filled with such events as greased pole climbing, pig chasing, fiddlers' contest, historical pageant and—oh yes, some 8000 people out panning for gold.

Tour No. 7
The Other Florida

Florida is bursting out with so much newness—real estate developments, industries, more and more hotels—that the unique, timeless qualities of the state are almost obscured. Yet here is the one truly sub-tropical corner of the United States, where the natural landscape is more comparable to the West Indies or South America than to other parts of our own country. Too few of Florida's millions of visitors realize that, in addition to the well known resort communities, they can stay at low cost in comfortable lodgings enveloped in pine forests, sharing the surroundings with beautiful rare birds and wildlife.

For a tour of three of the finest natural areas, drive first to Ocala National Forest, on Route 40, east of Ocala. Remember the charming story of *The Yearling,* by Marjorie Kinnan Rawlings? The novelist lived in this pine-scented woodland, and later the story was filmed here in natural setting. (A good idea is to re-read the book before your trip.) The best place to stay is at Juniper Springs Recreation Area, in the heart of the 360,000 acre forest. You can camp, rent a cabin, or bring your trailer; enjoy canoeing, swimming and fishing. Millions of bass, bream, shell crackers and related species are taken from its many lakes and streams. As a wildlife area, it has one of the South's largest deer herds, as well as protected animals and birdlife like the anhinga, armadillo, otter, alligator and many types of turtle.

From Ocala drive south on U. S. 301 through Central Florida, dotted with thousands of lakes, citrus groves and cattle ranches. To learn something of another phase of Florida's past, stop at the Dade Battlefield, Bushnell, the site of the Second Seminole War, which lasted from 1835 to 1841. The Seminoles, under Osceola, refused to be uprooted and moved West, or even to recognize the U. S. Government. At Bushnell, 110 soldiers under Major Francis Dade were ambushed and massacred. The area now contains a museum, monuments and picnic grounds.

This, too, is Florida's Vacationland: Juniper Springs, in Ocala National Forest, the pineland setting of Marjorie Kinnan Rawling's novel, The Yearling. *Facilities here (picnic tables, camping, cabins) are open all year.*

Inland from the popular Gulf Coast resort of Sarasota is Florida's largest state park, Myakka River (follow Routes 41, 72). In this vast wildlife sanctuary you can follow nature trails to see great wading birds, huge flocks of turkey, deer and raccoon. World travelers say that one section strongly resembles the African veldt. Several cabins, built of native palmetto and live oak, provide adequate if not plush accommodations ($30.90 per week, $5.15 per day). There also are campgrounds, boating, fishing in the river and lakes.

From Myakka, you have two routes on which to head south. One is U. S. 41 along the Gulf Coast, through the resort cities of Fort Myers and Naples. Should you follow the other route, State 29 through the Big Cypress Swamp, stop at Corkscrew Swamp Sanctuary, a huge stand of cypress now under supervision of the Audubon Society. Both routes lead to the Tamiami Trail, a highway which took twelve years to build, cutting straight across the Everglades and the Seminole country. The Reservation is actually north of the road but you will see Indians and their huts called "chickees."

The accessible heart of the Everglades, the "River of Grass," lies south of Miami in Everglades National Park. This is the second largest national park, exceeded in size only by Yellowstone. You can get a brief introduction to this subtropical wonderland at the Royal Palm Station, near the Park entrance at Homestead. But for an unusual experience, follow the new 39-mile road to Flamingo, deep in the park, and really explore its mangrove forests, hammocks and pine islands. Accommodations include 60-unit motel ($12–$14 double, winter; $8–$10, sum-

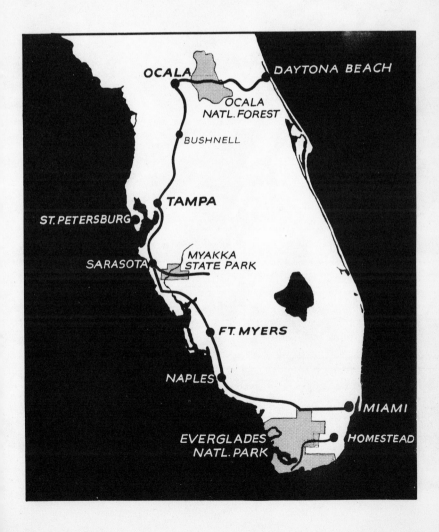

mer), campground and even a family-style houseboat for rent. Other facilities include restaurant, boating marina and picnic sites. There, at the shore of Florida Bay, you can witness flocks of white heron, roseate spoonbill and pink spoonbill in graceful flight—this is the haven and nesting ground of these rare wading birds. Join the guided nature walks, held in the evenings; at that hour, as one naturalist observes, "the animals are really whooping, hollering and crawling around."

Florida actually has every manner of accommodations, from plush resorts to motels, modest furnished apartments and campgrounds. Even along South Florida's golden strand during the period from May to November you can rent an ocean-front hotel room for $8–$10 double, a furnished apartment for $60 up weekly, a motel room for $4 or $5. At Miami Beach a couple could enjoy a week's vacation on a budget of $165, a family of four for about $250.

Tour No. 8
The Lincoln Country from Kentucky to Illinois

The Lincoln National Memorial Highway extends 425 miles, from the frontier farm cabin where Abraham Lincoln was born in obscurity to the tomb in which he rests in glory. Between them lie the milestones of Lincoln's adventurous life, with its successes and failures, its humor, tragedy, romance — the transformation of a backwoodsman to a President.

The route through the Lincoln Country starts at the Sinking Spring Farm, outside Hodgenville, Kentucky, where Thomas and Nancy Hanks Lincoln, a struggling frontier couple, brought their son into the world in 1809. The tiny single-window log cabin is preserved within a marble memorial building, while the surrounding land of the National Historical Park shows the Lincoln farm much as it was, complete with the Sinking Spring, the Lincolns' main water supply, and the ancient boundary oak tree. The Lincolns, however, were not to live here long. Before Abe was two years old they moved to Knob Creek, about ten miles northeast. Many of the scenes of Lincoln's childhood in and around Hodgenville are well marked.

While you are still on the trail of Abraham Lincoln in Kentucky,

Good catch! A pair of sizable warsaw groupers well under control at Miami's Pier 5.

The Lincoln Trail: from Hodgenville, Kentucky.

detour your course to Louisville, to visit the Farmington mansion on Bardstown Road (10 to 5 except Mondays, Sundays 2 to 5; 50¢). Lincoln came here in 1841 as a guest of Joshua Speed, who had been his closest friend in Springfield. Farmington, built in 1810 from a design by architect Thomas Jefferson, deserves recognition in its own right as a reminder of Kentucky's heritage, though it now stands at the junction of energetic expressways.

In 1816 Thomas Lincoln and his family headed westward into the wilderness, ferrying the Ohio River and settling on a farm near Gentry-ville, Indiana. His schooling at an end, Lincoln worked on a farm for 25 cents a day and, at 16, operated a ferry across the Ohio River. Then he helped take a flatboat of produce downstream to New Orleans.

Today, near Lincoln City, the state of Indiana preserves both the site of the farm and the burial place of his mother, who died in her middle thirties. Lincoln State Park, 1500 acres of gently sloping wooded knoll, has facilities for camping and swimming. Nearby are two other points of interest. The unique village of Santa Claus, a children's park, displays some of Lincoln's poems along with its toys, animals, and figures of Santa Claus. At Rockport, on a bluff above the winding Ohio, the Lincoln Pioneer Village contains 17 reconstructed cabins, including replicas of the Lincoln home, the Old Pigeon Baptist Church and pioneer schoolhouse.

But the Lincolns moved onward in 1830, when Abe was 21, crossing the Wabash at Vincennes to the Illinois prairies. About 250 miles of the Lincoln National Memorial Highway are in Illinois, the state where Lincoln rose to maturity and greatness. After helping his father build a new cabin, he left for New Salem to make his way in the world. The six years at New Salem were the turning point in his career. He clerked in a store, tried his hand in business and failed, served as town postmaster, left awhile as captain in the Black Hawk War, loved Ann Rutledge but lost her to death. Through his adversities he found his path to the study of law and government. Now New Salem State Park, the "Lincoln Village," is an authentic reproduction of the town as Lincoln knew it, complete with shops, cabins, tavern, and school, all furnished in detail. Even the Wagon Wheel, a rustic restaurant below the hill from the village, blends with the setting. Early American

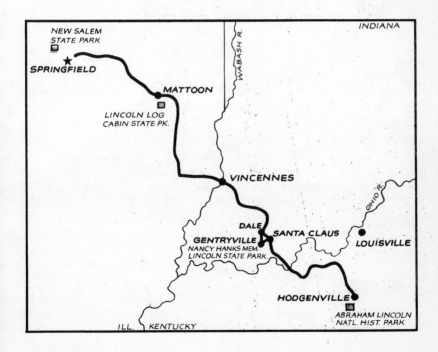

atmosphere is also a feature of the New Salem Lodge ($7–$9 double), just outside the park. An unusual feature at the park late in August is the presentation of the play *Abe Lincoln in Illinois* by the Abe Lincoln Players of Springfield, at the Kelso Hollow Theatre.

Springfield, Illinois' capital, holds many major Lincoln associations and points of interest. He lived here most of his mature years, practiced law, entered politics, and first took issue with Stephen Douglas. Even when he was President, Springfield was his home. At the unpretentious Lincoln Home, at Eighth and Jackson Streets, the only home he ever owned, visitors see many of the original furnishings used by the President, his wife, Mary Todd Lincoln, and their children. The Lincoln Tomb, in Oak Ridge Cemetery, north of the city, is an inspiring marble structure. The old state capitol, now the County Court House, is rich in Lincoln lore, for he served in the legislature and delivered here his famous "house divided against itself" speech. Have lunch or dinner at the Country House or Southern Air.

Cities and villages named for Lincoln are in every part of the country and the world, but only this three-state span, the distance between Hodgenville and Springfield, can ever be known as the Lincoln Country. In traveling the Lincoln National Memorial Highway, the story of a great figure in history becomes understandable in simple human terms.

Tour No. 9

Michigan's Upper Peninsula to Isle Royale

Roads and bridges don't exactly alter geography, but they do render it accessible. Where roads fail to penetrate, bridges, or causeways, succeed. Michigan's Upper Peninsula, a curious fragment of Great Lakes geography, is such a case.

The new discovery of the Upper Peninsula is due largely to the completion of the Mackinac Straits Bridge, a $100 million suspension structure, crossing the four-mile wide straits between Lake Michigan and Lake Huron. The bridge replaces ferries in service since 1923 and for the first time directly links Michigan's two peninsulas.

A new ferry fills an important role, too, in reaching Isle Royale National Park, on the largest island in Lake Superior, where the principal activities are fishing, boating and hiking, and the loudest noise is the purr of an outboard motor.

To a marble tomb at Springfield, Illinois.

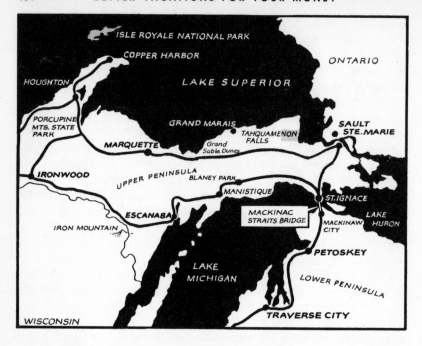

The Upper Peninsula is one tremendous piece of real estate, containing nearly nine million acres of forestland, more than 4000 inland lakes, and 1700 miles of shoreline along three of the Great Lakes—everything it takes for tomorrow's mass playground. But see it now, this year. Include it in your itinerary if you are driving across the northern tier of states. The Upper Peninsula has resort communities, drives along the inland sea, iron and copper mines, historic sites dating to the explorations of Pere Marquette.

From St. Ignace, at the northern side of the Mackinac Straits Bridge (toll $3.25, car and passengers), you can follow Route 2, skirting the shore of Lake Michigan to resorts, lumber centers, and fishing lakes in the vicinity of Blaney Park and Manistique. At Escanaba, where the Upper Peninsula State Fair is held every August, have luncheon at the House of Ludington. Iron Mountain, farther west, is gaining popularity as both a summer resort and winter sports center. At Ironwood, on the Wisconsin border, you will find one of the prettiest drives in the state, along the Black River for 17 miles as it passes four waterfalls to Lake Superior.

Spanning the straits: the four-mile bridge to the Upper Peninsula.

Out of the locks, an ore carrier steams through Sault Ste. Marie back to the open waters of the inland sea.

The northern portion of the Upper Peninsula has many distinctive features, more than a few still a little beyond reach. Try counting the number of ships passing through the locks of Sault Ste. Marie, one of the world's busiest water arteries, at the eastern end of the peninsula. Heading west, be sure to visit Tahquamenon Falls, in the midst of a virgin forest, another type of the peninsula's inspiring scenery. The Grand Sable Dunes and the red sandstone Pictured Rocks on Munising Bay are two spectacles of unique natural beauty along the indented coast. At Marquette, a popular headquarters for deep-sea trolling, eat at the Chalet, on the road to Negaunee.

The famous copper country of the Keweenaw Peninsula extends upward into Superior. At Houghton, the museum of the Michigan College of Mining and Technology houses one of the world's largest mineral displays. At Copper Harbor, the northernmost point on the peninsula, Fort Wilkins State Park preserves a restored remote army post of the last century.

From Houghton you can travel aboard the *Ranger III,* a new 100-passenger motor ship, to Isle Royale National Park, an 800-square-mile scenic wilderness island. The new one-million-dollar vessel makes the 75-mile trip in five hours, two hours less than the former crossing time of smaller vessels.

Boating enthusiasts can transport their own boats from the mainland or rent them on the island ($4 daily, you bring the motor).

Isle Royale is 45 miles long and nine miles across at its widest. Over 80 miles of foot trails lead to inland lakes, ruins of ancient copper mines and vantage points to observe wildlife. The most prominent trail extends 34 miles from Rock Harbor at the northeast end to Washington Harbor at the southwest; it is lined with campsites (shelter, fireplace, table, toilet). Arrange a combination trip, one way by boat, the other on the trail.

Besides the campsites, accommodations are available at Rock Harbor Lodge ($24 double, with meals), Windigo Inn ($18 double, with meals) and at new housekeeping cabins ($60 a week for family of four) at Rock Harbor. Reservations are advisable for the short mid-June to August season. Bring warm but informal clothing. Once you reach Isle Royale there is no place to go dressed up.

Tour No. 10
New Lakes, Old Hills in the Ozarks

The Ozarks are not the most lavish vacation area—nor the most expensive. The wooded hills and lake shores of southern Missouri, Arkansas, and Oklahoma are dotted with resorts specializing in family vacationing at extremely moderate cost. They also offer fishing and travel off the beaten track hard to surpass at any price. A couple can spend a week at an attractive resort, meals included, for about $125, a family of four for under $200.

As a vacation area, the Ozarks are only beginning to come into their own. They draw mostly from nearby middlewestern areas, but better roads are making them more widely accessible and new accommodations lend modern touch to match.

The Ozarks are a land of rugged hills, deep hollows, large artificial lakes, and swift-running streams. The tempo of living is a little slower than elsewhere, which suits the local people fine. Those colorful folk like their hills best and are as much at ease traveling in "johnboats" over the waterways as in automobiles over the roads.

Fishing is one of the great attractions, for visitor and native alike. Tremendous lakes, behind power dams, have won thousands of outdoorsmen and outdoor families as enthusiasts. The largest lake, the Lake of the Ozarks, is 129 miles long, with an indented, twisting shoreline of 1300 miles—and that's more shoreline than Lake Michigan. Its 60,000 acres are home to, and a happy hunting ground for largemouthed bass, walleye pike, giant-size crappie, channel cat, and white bass.

Farther south, lakes like Taneycomo, Clearwater, Grand, Gibson, Wapello, Bull Shoals, Norfork, Tenkiller, and Table Rock Reservoir, the newest, are abundant with smallmouth and largemouth bass, crappie, walleye, black perch, sunfish, and channel cat. These lakes offer more than fishing; in one month at Bull Shoals 8000 boats were rented, to indicate the way things go. Ozark areas also offer fine horseback riding, golf, and other sports.

Float fishing, on streams like the Current, White, and Gasconade, attracts expert fishermen from all parts of the country. The object is to float downstream, casting all the way—and on these winding streams you are likely to end a mile from your starting point! The daily rate is

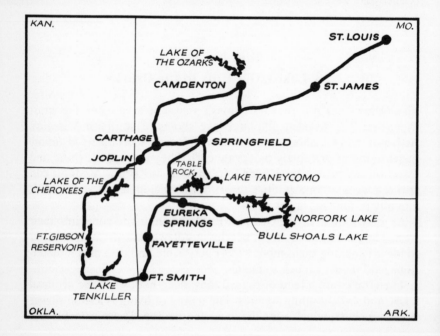

Bull Shoals Dam and Lake, completed in 1952, a promising Ozark resort center, with a 1000-mile shoreline and almost 15 boat dock areas.

modest: $15 for boat, guide, and lunch. The real thrill in float fishing is to overnight on the river. Usually there is no need to carry anything but your fishing gear. The outfitter provides the rest—a "commissary" boat goes ahead to prepare lunch at a prearranged point, and then to pitch camp by the time the day's fishing is done. The rate, including meals, camp cook, and guide: $25 a day.

An unusual recreational park in the Ozarks is 1600-acre Maramec, near St. James, Missouri. It was endowed by a lady of means, Mrs. Lucy Wortham James, to "keep the natural beauty unmarred for the enjoyment of the people." The tract includes a fresh-water spring (averaging 93 million gallons daily), fishing pond and streams, picnic tables, the remains of a historic iron furnace, and a small wildlife refuge. It is intended for lasting use as a recreational area and wildlife sanctuary.

Springfield and Joplin are the principal gateways to the southern Ozarks from Missouri, but Eureka Springs, Arkansas, is probably the

best-known resort, a curious little place of winding streets climbing steep hills. There are many other attractive communities, like Fayette-ville, where the University of Arkansas is located; Mountain Home, on Lake Norfork; Branson and Rockaway Beach on Taneycomo; and lesser known places back in the "hollers." The Taneycomo area is the setting of Harold Bell Wright's story, "Shepherd of the Hills." Re-read it to add perspective to your sightseeing. Hollister, south of the Lake, is an unusual community. All its buildings are English design, a con-trast to the surrounding mountain cabins.

Good food, country style, is an Ozark feature too. Menus are not what you would call elegant, but there is no dearth of wholesome cured ham, fried chicken, hot biscuits and cornbread, jams and preserves made from homegrown fruits. There is entertainment to match—a lively Saturday night square dance with a traditional fiddler calling. Earthly? Yes. Fun? Verily!

Tour No. 11
Deep Dixie, Natchez, and New Orleans

Many roads lead to the Lower Mississippi Valley and New Orleans, but once there was only one sensible route from the East, the river. Flat boats started from Pittsburgh, floated down to St. Louis, and kept right on going. Getting back was another, more complicated story, until steam-powered paddle wheelers arrived on the scene.

The closest thing to a main road was the Natchez Trace. It had begun as a chain of Indian trails, was used in turn by the French, English, and Spanish explorers, then by the Americans. Before the steamboat, men from Kentucky, who floated downstream, walked back on the Trace—a long walk.

With the development of river traffic and other routes, the Trace was abandoned and, except for a street name in Nashville, largely forgotten until our time and the establishment of the Natchez Trace National Parkway. Though still under construction, it has already earned its way as a scenic, recreational route, running diagonally across Tennes-see, Alabama, and Mississippi. About one third of its 450 miles is complete, mostly in Mississippi, but new sections will open continually during the next few years.

Eden Falls, in Lost Valley, near Ponca, Arkansas, a touch of Ozark beauty off the beaten path.

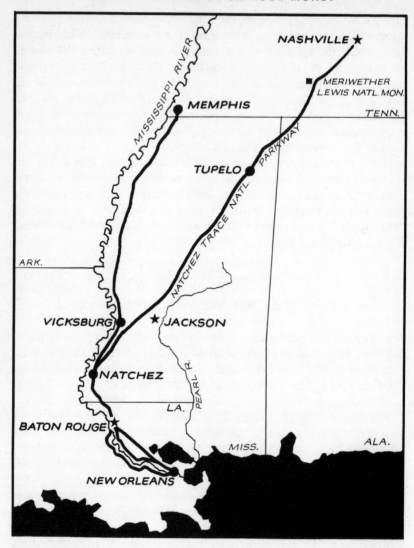

A number of recreation areas and vestiges of the old Trace lend interest to the trip. Near Hohenwald in Tennessee the Meriwether Lewis National Monument marks the spot where the great trailblazer died a suicide. In Mississippi, the Tupelo-Baldcypress Swamp and the Pearl River (once a main navigation channel) are scenic finds. Mount Locust, one of the "newest" developments, is a restoration of a pioneer home and tavern. And the Trace ends, as you might expect, at another tavern, Connelly's by name, now headquarters of the Natchez Garden Club. In time, travelers along this venerable route from Nashville to Natchez will be able to view cotton fields, cotton gins, sugar cane and sugar plantations, but even now the Trace offers a great deal.

Other roads lead to deepest Dixie too. Driving from Memphis through the Mississippi Delta to New Orleans you arrive midway at Vicksburg, one of the most zestful little cities of them all. Here you get the feeling of the roistering, romantic old riverboat days, particularly when you board the *Sprague,* the mightiest vessel ever to sail the Mississippi, now docked permanently at the levee front (admission, 25¢; children under 12, 10¢).

Vicksburg's principal attraction is the National Military Park, forming a crescent around the city. The battle line, now 30 miles of scenic roadway, is well marked. Here in 1863, Vicksburg became the "Gibraltar of the Confederacy," besieged by land and sea. It was the Rebels' last stronghold on the River, the vital link with Louisiana, Arkansas and Texas—and it could not be allowed to fall. But Grant, moving his army through swamp and marsh without communications or supplies, fighting two separate Confederate armies, ringed the city with firepower and forced it to surrender. The date of his triumph, July 4, 1863, was almost simultaneous with the Union Victory at Gettysburg.

The Old Courthouse, where Grant ran up the Union flag, has become a museum of fascinating Southern memorabilia, its most unusual feature the old courtroom itself with its high (23 feet) ceiling, wide cypress flooring, swiveling jurors' seats, and old iron grills (admission, 50¢; children under 12, 10¢). Don't miss the U. S. Corps of Engineers Experiment Station, which conducts free guided tours; you will see small-scale underwater explosions and models of famous waterways. Stop for lunch at the Old Southern Tea Room (try a potent Vicksburg Voodoo cocktail and river catfish with hushpuppies or trout amandine), or at Tuminello's (for oyster bienville or lasagna).

Vicksburg is liveliest during Pilgrimage season in March, when camellia and azalea gardens are in bloom and ladies in hoop skirts escort visitors through two ante bellum homes, Anchuca ($1) and Planters Hall (50¢). That month the Showboat Players stage "Gold in the Hills," Gay Nineties fare aboard the Sprague, ($2).

Natchez, farther south, is on the same river, but differs from Vicksburg as much as San Francisco does from Los Angeles. Genteel, romantic, and lusty, Natchez still bears the aura of its heyday when

cotton kings built lavish mansions to symbolize frontier wealth and culture.

The ante bellum homes are beauties of architecture and interior furnishings. Approximately fifteen are open to visitors all year (9–5, 75¢–$1.00 each), but the most attractive period is the month of March, when the gardens are abloom and the weather ideal. The famed Natchez Pilgrimage, held throughout the month, includes guided tours to thirty homes, many not open any other time. The houses are divided into six groups; ʰour tickets for five houses, $4; for all thirty houses, $20.

During the Pilgrimage, reservations are advisable and lodging rates are higher. A wonderful place to stay is Stanton Hall ($8–$12), veritably a palace in its day; now it is headquarters of the Pilgrimage Garden Club and several rooms are rented to overnight guests. The Carriage House Restaurant on the grounds serves fine meals. Another mansion accepting guests is Hope Farm, the home of Mrs. Katherine Grafton Miller, the celebrated founder of the Natchez Pilgrimage.

Though Natchez is prettiest during spring, there is something to be said for summer, if you can take the heat. The Deep South is scarcely more humid than some northern cities; air conditioning makes life more liveable, and rates are lower.

On the way to New Orleans, stop at Baton Rouge to visit the towering Louisiana state capitol and the campus of Louisiana State University. From here the Airline Highway is the shortest route, but the least scenic. Two others, Routes 44 and 18, one on each side of the Mississippi, lead to points where you can climb the levee bank for a clear view of the broad river, then drive on through shaded oak groves, passing languid bayous and time-weathered plantation houses.

New Orleans is the kind of place where you can spend a large bankroll happily. But you can be happy on a low budget too—for the best of New Orleans is free. The French Quarter is so compact that you can cover it all on foot; the famous Cabildo is a public building, St. Louis Cathedral still in use as a church, and the only charge at the French Market is the price of your coffee and doughnuts.

You may not realize this, but you can stay at a guest house in the Quarter. Lamothe House ($9–$12 double) is outstanding, furnished with antiques dating to the early 1800's when it was built. You'll enjoy the petit dejeuner in the dining room and afternoon cafe Brulot (black, with spices and liquor) in the palmetto-shaded courtyard.

When Grant took Vicksburg, he established his headquarters in this courthouse, now a museum of southern memorabilia.

From here you have flavorful New Orleans at your fingertips on streets with old French names like Rue Royale and Rue Chartres, lined with cherished, weathered buildings, and on Bourbon Street, where Dixieland jazz is heard nightly. Treat yourself to dinner at one of New Orleans' famous restaurants, but note that Galatoire's and Antoine's are open only until 9 P.M., Brennan's until midnight.

Tour No. 12
Western Slope of the Colorado Rockies

Southwestern Colorado is one of the lesser known vacation areas of the West, or even of its own state, where Estes Park and Colorado Springs have been pre-eminent for years. Yet the lofty, cool San Juan Basin and its surroundings are a treasurehold of mountain scenery, and generally less expensive. A couple can get by for a week's vacation on about $110, a family of four on $160; the average family will spend about $220. Campers will cut their costs in half, at least.

The southwestern region is covered with national forests, the Gunnison, Uncompahgre, Montezuma, and San Juan, and there is no shortage of outdoors elbow room. The mountain towns have had a fabled past, with vestiges still evident of the lusty mining days of the 1880's.

For a tour of the area, start from Grand Junction, which has boomed into a uranium mining center. If you decide to try your luck, you can rent equipment and geiger counter here and strike out into the wilds. For vacation purposes, however, follow Route 50 southeast to Montrose and the Black Canyon of the Gunnison National Monument, one of America's great natural spectacles. The rims of the narrow, deep gorge are only 1300 feet apart at their closest, yet the distance straight down is 1700 to 2400 feet. The name Black Canyon comes from the color of the sombre rocks and granite. A highway leads to observation points and campgrounds overlooking the ribbon-like Gunnison River.

Returning to Montrose, drive south on Route 550 to Alpine-like Ouray, in the heart of the San Juan Range.

Ouray, ringed entirely by snowy peaks 12,000 to 14,000 feet high, is the starting point of jeep trips over old pack-horse trails. On the way

The mansion at Audubon State Park, St. Francisville, Louisiana, where John James Audubon came to be a tutor, but turned instead to his calling and completed 32 of his Birds of America series.

up the route passes Camp Bird Mine, where Tom Walsh struck it rich enough to buy his daughter, Evelyn Walsh McLean, the famous Hope Diamond; along with others in the isolated high canyons it is still operating, sending out rich ore every day. But the trail leads upward, to some of the highest accessible points in America.

Even ordinary motoring in these mountains opens spectacular vistas. The best-known road, the Million Dollar Highway (so-called because it reportedly cost a million dollars a mile to build) between Ouray and Durango, literally carved out of the mountainside, leads through deep canyons and gorges.

Ouray, ringed by the San Juan Mountains, is the starting point of jeep trips scaling the heights, above mines like the famous Camp Bird, to the 14,000-foot rooftop of the Colorado Rockies.

If you like railroads, you'll love to ride the Silverton, the last regularly scheduled narrow-gauge passenger train, operated during the summer to give a sentimental glimpse of those rugged days when the railroad joined remote, wealthy mining towns with the outside world. Its puffing, coal-burning engine and brightly colored coaches chug and click through the canyons and alongside high mountain streams—an experience unmatched. The train leaves Durango at 9:15 A.M., spends two hours in Silverton, returns to Durango about 6:15 P.M. Fare: $3 round trip.

As for Silverton, it looks authentically western even by Hollywood standards; half a dozen top movies (including *Viva Zapata, Run for Cover, Outcasts of Poker Flat*) have been shot here. Silverton's Grand Imperial was a palatial hotel in the silver boom of the '80s. Recently restored and modernized, the Grand Imperial is a lively place to stay (double $7–$9).

The Cliff Palace, the largest and best preserved of the Stone Age dwellings in Mesa Verde National Park.

Near the Four Corners, at Colorado's southwestern border, are the great ruins of Mesa Verde National Park, on U. S. 160 from Durango, preserving the thousand-year-old cliff dwellings of America's stone-age civilization. The inhabitants of this stark, remote region of cliffs and mesas are believed to have made their way originally from Asia across the Bering Straits, finally coming here to build their homes beyond the reach of warlike tribes.

The Park is well designed for a compact presentation of highlights, but allow two days, longer if you want to hike or ride the trails. Start at the Park museum, where dioramas depict Mesa Verde in its various stages, then join a tour conducted by a Park ranger-archaeologist. The Cliff Palace is the most famous of the ruins, with over 200 living rooms and 23 kivas (ceremonial chambers). The kiva, as the naturalist points out, was the inviolate sanctuary of the men, open to women only when there was cleaning to be done or when their men called them to bring food. Near Park Headquarters both campgrounds and concession-operated Spruce Tree Lodge (double, $4.50–$8.75) provide accommodations.

Don't miss the evening talk given by an archaeologist at the camp-fire in summer. Evenings at this elevation are cool, so carry a sweater or wrap.

Tour No. 13

Yellowstone and the Tetons: Crowds in Open Spaces

Visualize more than a million people visiting Yellowstone and the Grand Tetons during a summer season of three short months—no less than 15,000 entering the gates of Yellowstone every day.

There is surely no lack of company. Yet there are places in both these national parks where you can be enveloped in natural scenery, undisturbed, unmindful of the throngs or your nearest neighbor. Those who come in the peak period and must either sleep in their cars or travel to the nearest motel vacancy only wish they had known!

Yellowstone is so large (3470 square miles) that, apart from camp-grounds, it can accommodate 10,000 persons a night in everything from modest cabins at $1.50 to hotel rooms at $15. And at the Grand Tetons, the new Colter Bay development, with its cabins and spacious camp sites, is designed entirely for economical family vacationing, as a supplement to other facilities elsewhere in the park.

To visit properly these magnificent regions in northwestern Wyoming—Yellowstone extends into Montana and Idaho as well—requires forethought, preparation, and reservations in advance. You cannot, except early or late in the season, expect to arrive and with certainty find accommodations in your price range.

But overnighting is only part of it. With all the sights and activities at Yellowstone and the Tetons, allow enough time for your visit. Those who travel thousands of miles to get here and then are content to motor through have missed the best of it.

At Yellowstone, the oldest national park, the Grand Loop encom-passes noted features like Old Faithful, Yellowstone Lake, the Grand Canyon of the Yellowstone River, and Mammoth Hot Springs. But to understand and appreciate them, and the animals, trees, and flowers, take advantage of the lectures, nature walks, twilight wildlife search, and the evening programs. Spend a few days—not hours—in Yellow-stone. Absorb more than the developed Loop; by car you can drive

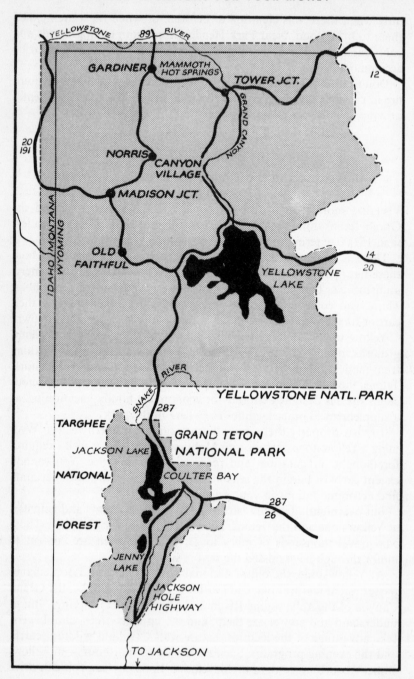

Boating on Jackson Lake, in the shadow of double-domed Mount Moran.

the pleasant old Tower Falls Road and other roads off the beaten path, by foot or horseback you can follow well-marked trails through peaceful woodlands.

Yellowstone's sixteen improved campgrounds are free, operated on a first-come, first-served basis. The most economical accommodations are tourist cabins, partially furnished, renting from $2.75 for a family of four, plus rental charge for bedding and cooking utensils. These are very plain facilities, but others, in graduated prices, offer more. At the new Canyon Village of 500 modern motel units the rate for a family of four is $17. It is open May 15–October 1. Reservations for all accommodations are accepted after March 1. Write Yellowstone Park Company, Yellowstone, Wyoming.

A plea for the bears: These wild creatures are intended to be observed from a distance. To feed the bears turns them into pitiable beggars of the road—and in time into demanding, dangerous beggars. The bear that attacks humans is sentenced by Park officials to be

executed. Help save the lives of Yellowstone bears by giving them a wide berth—and do not feed them.

In the Grand Tetons, the Colter Bay area represents the newest kind of national park vacation facility. The campground includes 250 individual sites, each marked and numbered, with a specific size—either 40 by 60 feet or 30 by 70 feet; each has its own cooking grate, table, and benches. Located in the central service area are stores, cafeteria, bath building, and automatic laundry. The 125 cabins, spacious, comfortable, and rustic, are near the stores and cafeteria too; they do not have housekeeping facilities. They rent from $10 to $18. Note this latest addition (summer, 1960) at Colter Bay: a number of new type "housekeeping tents." They're set on concrete flooring with two sides of logs, bed bunks under canvas roof and fireplace directly outside. Check for rates—they will be reasonable.

Other accommodations in the park are the Jackson Lake Lodge of 300 rooms, most in cottages, and the distinctive Jenny Lake Lodge for a limited number of guests. For reservations write Grand Teton Lodge Company, at 209 Post Street, San Francisco 8, California (before May 9) or at Grand Teton National Park, Wyoming (summer address). No matter where you stay, have a drink at the Stockade Room at the Jackson Lake Lodge, furnished in the period when Jackson Hole was the crossroads of the North American fur trade.

Grand Teton National Park is best identified by the dramatic wall of the snow-capped Teton mountains, but this spectacular view should be only an introduction to enjoying the park in its fullness. You can hike, climb mountains, ride, fish, swim, go boating. One of the most memorable experiences is the six-hour float trip on the Snake River through Jackson Hole Valley, enjoyable for all ages ($10). Or you may rent a boat at Colter Bay or one of the smaller lakes.

Use your car to explore the whole area. The new Jackson Hole Highway, along the east side of the park, offers some of the finest mountain views in the country. Drive to the little city of Jackson, 30 miles south, a zestful spot worthy of the Jackson Hole tradition, and stop in at the Wort Hotel, the center of activity. Both Yellowstone and the Tetons are surrounded by national forests. Driving through Targhee National Forest in Idaho you get another spectacular perspective of the Teton Range. Targhee, in the Island Park country, contains thrilling sights of its own, including Cave Falls and the Grand Canyon of the Snake River.

Twice Niagara's height, the Lower Falls of the Yellowstone River splash into spray and mist.

Tour No. 14

Reno, Squaw Valley and the Sierras

Squaw Valley, the scene of the 1960 Winter Olympics, is unquestionably the new showplace of the Sierras and the Olympics rank as the greatest event in these parts since the discovery of gold in 1848. However, when you travel this way plot a tour of the Sierras as a region, covering both California and Nevada. In all directions are national forestland, spectacular scenery, and old mining towns with vestiges of the Gold Rush days.

Consider Reno as a base. Basically, the cost of vacationing here or in Las Vegas, or any other gambling town, is not high. You get a pretty good bargain in such items as bed and board as an invitation to the gaming tables and slot machinery. There is a technique in trying your luck and staying solvent, as we shall see presently, and if you accept it you can enjoy a three-day weekend for as low as $50 a couple or a week for about $125.

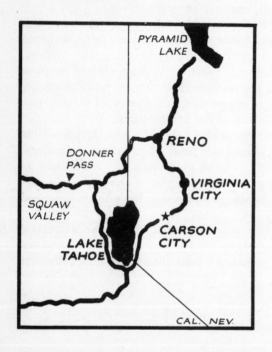

With the recent four-laning of Route 40 across the mountains, Reno is only about five hours drive from San Francisco and only one hour from Squaw Valley. For a tour through the heart of the region, follow this route:

Drive west from Reno on Route 40. As you climb up to Donner Lake and Donner Summit, you get a sense of the magnitude of the Sierras, a tremendous range which extends as an unbroken north-south chain for 250 miles, ranging in altitude from 3,000 feet upward to 14,000 feet. The Donner Monument recalls a tragic episode in Western expansion, almost incomprehensible in our era of mobility and convenience; but at this point in 1846 the pioneer Donner party, trapped in winter snows, resorted to cannibalism for survival.

Turn south on Route 89 to Squaw Valley, a natural amphitheatre a mile wide and two miles long, the site of the Winter Olympics in the United States in 1932, involving more than 1,000 athletes from 34 nations—the largest international competition in the history of winter sports. Of the 6,000 acres of land carved out of the wilderness, 1,000 are remaining as a permanent State Park and outdoor sports center.

The main building is the 11,000-seat Ice Arena, enclosed on three sides with the open south side facing the speed skating rink and ski jumps. You'll also see the Olympic Flame and Monument, multi-colored dormitories of Olympic Village, Speed Skating Oval and double chair lifts—possibly by the time of your visit these will be in use for summer sightseeing, as well as for skiers' use in winter. Plan to stop for lunch or refreshments at one of the lounges or restaurants.

Squaw Valley overlooks Lake Tahoe, which you reach in a few minutes by continuing on Route 89. Tahoe, the blue gem of the Sierras, is ringed with green forests rising to snowy peaks 3,000 feet above it. It is the largest lake in North America over 6,000 feet in elevation and its 100-mile shoreline is dotted with beaches, hotels and resorts. About two-thirds are in California, one-third in Nevada. Emerald Bay, on the southern shore, is an excellent state park with facilities for boating, camping and fishing. Nevada Beach, on the Nevada side, operated by Douglas County, is a similar development. Remember, however, that Nevada has the gambling shore, and you can do this in style at luxurious Cal-Neva Lodge.

South of Tahoe you can follow Route 50 to old mining towns like Placerville, formerly known as Hangtown, and Route 49 through the heart of the Mother Lode gold country. However, to complete the loop to Reno, drive to Carson City, Nevada's state capital; then to Virginia City, once the wealthiest place on the continent, where the fabled Comstock Lode yielded more than $750 million. Crumbling

glories are evident in all its buildings—the opera house, saloons, faded mansions of the nabobs. The best souvenir you can buy is a copy of the Territorial Enterprise, published by that worldly, enterprising character, Lucius Beebe. This is probably the only weekly newspaper in the world with paid advertisements from Antoine's in New Orleans, the St. Regis in New York and the Pump Room in Chicago (as well as the Delta Cafe, Virginia City's "favorite sluicing rendezvous").

Back to Reno and gambling. Of course you are going to gamble. Everyone does, including the natives. Slot machines are in every nook and cranny of every conceivable establishment, except the schools, banks, churches, and government buildings. Even the housewife, after she buys her groceries, invests her change in the supermarket's slot machine. The way to have fun is to face the fact that you are not a professional gambler (unless, of course, you are one) and to play for kicks, not for keeps. This means you say to yourself, "How much can I invest?" If it's $5, or whatever the amount proves to be, you put that amount in your gambling pocket and move all the rest to the safe-keeping pocket. Or you give the bankroll to your wife—unless you are already holding hers!

The secret to intelligent amateur gambling is the matter of pacing. Think of yourself as a distance runner who does not start with a sprint. You want to stay with it, have fun, and see if you can win enough to buy yourself a Christmas present out of season. So you go into a gambling place like Harolds Club, which is the largest in the world, or Harrah's, another sizable establishment. These places are operated for everybody who wants to gamble anything from a dime to a thousand dollars. The experts here know who are the biggest gamblers (Californians) and the smallest (New Englanders). Before you jump in, study the games. If you are not versed in blackjack or craps or roulette, find out first.

No matter how much you start with, divide it into small units—dimes, let us say. Play dimes in the slot machine until you win: with small units you can ride out a losing streak till it turns. If you win, you can increase your stakes until you are playing with silver dollars. Every time you make the amount of your original investment, that $5, take it out and put it on the safe-keeping side. That is your profit; yet you are still operating with your original investment. Most important: don't dip beyond that stake. It is quite possible to end up a winner

The roulette table at Reno, where a little caution goes a long way.

because the ethical gambling business establishments will give you every break. They want you to have fun and come back; their earnings are based on a high-volume operation rather than a high take per customer.

Gambling is not the only way to have fun in Reno. The Truckee River runs through the town and you can cast your line in the center of the city. Ten-pound trout have been taken in the city limits!

If you want to see something quite different, even for this section, travel 45 miles north to Pyramid Lake, with a jutting rock formation in its center and a background of desert and mountains.

Tour No. 15
The Oregon Coast

Oregon has what the Nation needs more of—accessible, unspoiled beachfront. Its 400-mile coastline is enviably undefiled in an era when uncontrolled development and the neon plague have altered, if not ruined, most other places.

The sandy beaches, rocky headlands and sheltered coves are many things to many users. Thirty-five state parks and forest camps provide low cost seashore camping ($1 per night for tent site, $1.50 for car and trailer), picnicking and swimming. At the right places, the fishing for cutthroat trout and chinook salmon may be the finest on the Continent. History-minded travelers, especially enthusiasts of Lewis and Clark, can pursue the pioneers' course to the Pacific. And even rockhounds have a field day in digging for agates and semi-precious stones.

The Oregon Coast Highway, U. S. 101, is the kind of road that transforms driving into touring. It leads through seaside towns, alongside sand dunes, colorful shrubs and flowers, roaring surf breaking against the cliffs. The highway is never far from the ocean, though your view may be blotted out occasionally if a fog drifts in.

A couple can manage a week's vacation trip along the Coast for about $115, a family of four for $160. Campers will do it for less. Following is a suggested itinerary and some of the highlights:

Assume you're starting at Brookings, just above the California border, and driving north. One of the first main points of interest will be Gold Beach, at the mouth of the Rogue River. Just above here, at Wedderburn, you can take an exciting 32-mile trip up the Rogue on the mail boat to Agness (round trip $4, children $2). Continuing north on 101, Humbug Mountain, elevation 1748 feet, is the highest point on the Coast. At Coos Bay and North Bend, both large ship-

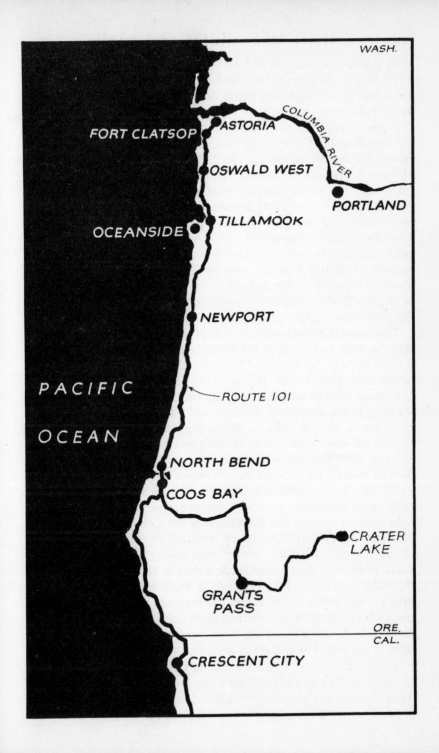

ping ports, you can tour lumber mills and arrange deep sea fishing trips. Stop at the plant in the center of North Bend to watch craftsmen turn and polish souvenirs made of myrtlewood. These articles are really handsome, although not cheap.

Approaching Newport, you'll see Heceta Head, about midway up the length of the Coast, a spectacular mariner's landmark and lighthouse, 520 feet above the sea. Devil's Elbow State Park nestles next to the beach. At Seal Rocks you may catch a look at sea lions basking off shore. You enter Newport over a high cantilever bridge across Yaquina Bay, one of many graceful spans which carry the highway over rivers and inlets along this rugged coast. Newport itself is a growing center of recreation and industry with a half dozen state parks, spectacular scenic and ocean views close by. In spring, if you stop at Boiler Bay Wayside, you may even see schools of whales off shore. Newport is a crab and oyster center, and one of the few places in the world where rock oysters are found abundantly. The port bustles with sport cruisers, commercial fishing vessels and lumber shipping.

Tillamook, farther north, is another colorful town, center of a rich dairy section and home of the Tillamook cheese. Free tours are conducted through the Modern Cheese Factory daily 9 to 5. A good spot to eat is the New Victory House on the north side of the city.

Oswald West State Park, near Manzanita, is one of the most outstanding beach areas, with excellent surf fishing, swimming, clamming, agate caves and camping on Short Sand Beach. The highway here rounds the steep rock face of Neahkahnie Mountain, 700 feet above the sea, 1000 feet below the mountain summit. Appropriately, this park is named for Oswald West, Oregon's Governor from 1911 to 1915, who safeguarded the shoreline for perpetual public benefit, rather than permitting it to be exploited commercially.

In nearing Astoria and the mouth of the Columbia River, stop to see newly designated Fort Clatsop National Memorial, reconstruction of the tiny palisaded log fort (50-foot square), built by Lewis and Clark to serve as their winter headquarters in 1805. One month before they had reached the Pacific Ocean in Washington State, but on this high ground above the mouth of the present Lewis and Clark River, the pioneers spent three months before starting their long trek eastward to St. Louis. The replica, with two long rows of rooms forming sides of the fort, was erected by local historical societies in 1955.

Astoria, the oldest English speaking city on the West Coast, was founded in 1811 as a fur trading post; the principal landmark is the Astor Column on Coxcomb Hill, 125 feet high with a 7-foot spiral frieze depicting early events. An observation platform affords a view of the wide river, mountains and the Ocean. Today Astoria is best known for its salmon and tuna fishing industries, and for sport fishing, at its best from August 1 to mid-September.

From here you can follow the Columbia River Highway inland to Portland or ferry across the River's wide estuary to Megler, in Washington State.

Or you can turn inland on the way north, and drive to Portland through Salem, Oregon's attractive capital. If you are not in a hurry, visit Silver Falls State Park, with 14 waterfalls, the highest over 175 feet. Portland is one of the country's most ideally located cities, on the Columbia River, in full view of mountain peaks. Despite its high latitude, it enjoys a mild climate, thanks to the Japanese current. Be sure to have a shell fish meal in Portland; try Dan and Louis Oyster Bar or Jake's Famous Crawfish.

The Exposition site, eight miles north near the crossing of the Columbia River by U. S. 99, covers 65 acres. The main exposition building is 11 acres under one roof, and adjacent to it a series of miniature settlements show life in Frontier Town, Lewis and Clark Village, Boom Town, and an operating logging camp. Portions of the Atomic Energy Commission display on the peaceful use of atomic energy have been moved from the Brussels World's Fair for the first showing in the United States. The International Trade Fair portion shows products from all over the world, and the International Garden of Tomorrow will feature new plant materials just being developed.

Eastward from Portland, the famous Columbia River Highway leads to Multnomah Falls, Bonneville Dam, where salmon swim upstream through the fish ladders, and Mount Hood, highest point in the state (11,245 feet) and a year-round vacation spot. Include a luncheon stop at the famous Timberline Lodge.

Eastern Oregon is sparsely settled, with cowboys, Indians, miners, and loggers reminiscent of old western days. The Pendleton Round-Up, held each September, is one of the country's top western rodeos. Hell's Canyon, where the Snake River forms the boundary between Oregon and Idaho, is the deepest gorge on the continent and thrilling boat trips are operated from Homestead to the canyon entrance.

Sundown at Oswald West State Park, Oregon.

Credit for the cartography in this book is gratefully acknowledged by the author to *Stephen Kraft*.

Credit for the photographs is gratefully acknowledged to the following organizations and individuals:

Air Force Museum, Dayton, Ohio
Arkansas Publicity and Parks Commission
Canadian Government Travel Bureau (Chris Lund)
City of Miami News Bureau
Colonial Williamsburg (Robert C. Lautman, David Brooks, George Beamish)
Eastman Kodak Company
Ford Motor Company
Kentucky Department of Information
Louisiana Department of Commerce and Industry
Michigan Tourist Council
Mississippi Agricultural and Industrial Board
National Park Service (Ralph H. Anderson, W. Verde Watson, Jean Speiser, Arthur Holmes, Warren Hamilton, Abbie Rowe, D. Moser)
New York State Department of Commerce
Oregon State Highway Department
Photolog (Rodney Morgan)
Portland Cement Association
Rhode Island Development Council
Lacy Ringgins, Aspen, Colorado
Savannah, Georgia, Chamber of Commerce (Al L'Heureux)
Tennessee Division of Information
Texas Oil Company (John Keller)
Thompson Pictures, Knoxville, Tennessee
Union Pacific Railroad Company
United States Forest Service (Clint Davis, Leland J. Prater, Bluford W. Muir, W. B. Alcorn)
United States Steel Corporation
Vicksburg, Mississippi, Chamber of Commerce
Ware County, Georgia, Chamber of Commerce
Robert F. Warner, Inc.
Marion Warren, Annapolis, Maryland